THE HARIM AND THE PURDAH

DANCING GIRL OF JEYPORE.

THE HARIM AND THE PURDAH

STUDIES OF ORIENTAL WOMEN

BY

ELIZABETH COOPER

ILLUSTRATED

NEW YORK

THE CENTURY COMPANY

Republished by Gale Research Company, Book Tower, Detroit, 1975

Library of Congress Cataloging in Publication Data

Cooper, Elizabeth, 1877-1945.
    The harim and the purdah.

    Reprint of the 1915 ed.
    1. Women in the East. 2. East–Social life and
customs. I. Title.
HQ1170.C77 1975   301.41'2'095   68-23147
ISBN 0-8103-3167-5

CONTENTS

6 CONTENTS

ILLUSTRATIONS

8   ILLUSTRATIONS

To face p. 9.

"TWO WOMEN SHALL BE GRINDING AT THE MILL."

INTRODUCTION

"What thou biddest
Unargued I obey. So God ordains;
God is *thy* law, thou mine: to know no more
Is woman's happiest knowledge, and her praise."

THIS is the creed of the woman of the East
to-day. It is the same as it has been for
centuries; it will continue the same for centuries
to come. Indeed, it is a question whether the
Oriental woman, with all her intellectual and
social advance which is already beginning, will
be able ever to free herself from those traditional
and inherent influences which have been wrought
into the very warp and woof of Eastern humanity.

The Eastern woman is primarily a tradi-
tionalist. She is more closely bound by hereditary tendency than the woman of the West.
One of her outstanding characteristics has lain
for years in her dependency and passive reliance
upon her husband for economic support and protection. Her very seclusion means to her, not
that which the word would connote to the
Westerner, slavery or imprisonment; to her it
is rather the mantle of protective care and
interest thrown over her by her lord and master.

It has helped to make her feminine, as it has naturally added to her inefficiency as far as any work is concerned that bears a similitude of masculine activity.

With the exception of the Burmese woman, and to an appreciable and growing extent the women of Japan, the Oriental woman has been influenced and moulded by her economic necessities. The Eastern attitude toward woman, which in general has been to keep her ignorant and to consider that her charms other than those relating to her physical attractions are minute, has brought about a feminine type peculiar to itself. The result is a woman who outside of the home has no power of gaining a livelihood, and who as a natural consequence has turned her whole thought, emotion, and imagination upon her domestic affairs. Furthermore, we find in such countries of the Orient as Burmah and Japan, where women are solving the problem of self-support, that they have also been able, not only to have greater freedom, but also, to a certain extent, they have demanded the right to choose their own mates and regulate the laws concerning their home life. For instance, in each of these countries the wife has the right of divorcing her husband—a right denied the woman of other Oriental lands. The property rights of women in these lands, where women are just beginning to be wage-earners, are also clearly set forth in their civil codes, giving justice to the women.

The realm of the Eastern woman is primarily the realm of the home. She has the true spirit of the bee; she considers the collective good of the household before her own. Her great vocation is to be a wife and mother. She attends personally to her household duties, and domestic service is to her not a disgrace. Her children are to her a veritable life-work. She looks after them personally, superintends their every act, and watches closely their development. Even the high lady of the East does not consider it demeaning to cook with her own hands that which she knows will appeal to the taste of her family. Cooking, indeed, is regarded as a fine art in the East, and recipes are handed down like heirlooms from mother to daughter along with the family jewels.

The Eastern woman is honoured by the honour of her household. It is her business to make it possible for her husband and her sons to advance, and she shines in the reflected light of their achievements. She has not been taught, neither has she any suspicion of the Western ambition to make name and fame for herself. There is a certain delight and satisfaction in living behind the veil which one can hardly appreciate from the Western point of view. That this Eastern feminine regards her success as domestic rather than social is abundantly proved to any one who lives intimately in touch with the women of these countries.

The one great cry which goes up from the

heart of every Oriental woman, regardless of place or station, in any home between Algiers and Tokio, is, " Give me sons ! " It is this desire for men-children, and the belief on the part of the woman that this is the primal and ultimate destiny of womanhood, that has made marriage the universal custom for all women throughout the East. Rarely indeed do you find an un-married woman. In India marriage is assured by betrothal in early childhood ; and even in those countries where education and Western influence are raising the age limit of marriages one finds no diminution in the general feeling that woman's world is the home, with her children about her.

This devotion to the purely domestic realm has left the woman a victim to ignorance, super-stition, and the many evils that follow in their train. One finds the same superstition working in the minds of the women in Cairo, in Calcutta, and in Peking. The Egyptian mother dresses her boy in rags to guard him from the baneful influence of the " evil eye," while the woman of China pierces her son's ears and places a ring therein, to deceive the gods and make them think he is a girl. The woman of Algiers will buy charms and magic symbols to bring her the blessing of motherhood, while the woman of Japan visits shrines and holy places, where her faith and superstition are traded upon by those who understand the weakness of their womenkind. She has so long been accustomed to rely upon her superstitions, her emotions, and to use her intuition in the place of a brain, that the present beginnings in education have been hampered. That, however, she will prove herself capable in the realm of mental training is proven by the fact that, especially in Egypt and in Japan, modern schools for girls are becoming really popular movements in the development of these countries. Every advance in the education of men adds to the possibility of intellectual emancipation for women.

During long ages Eastern women have been denied the right to think for themselves and have been compelled to feel their way emotionally, and their power to feel thus has become abnormally developed at the expense of their power to judge or reason. The woman of the Orient is a woman swayed by emotions, by the heart instead of by the intellect.

There is a logical line of connection to be traced among the modern women of the East. Her phases of development have been the inevitable outcome of influences to which she has been taught to submit as a duty. Her religious sense—the strong spiritual craving that is deep within the heart of all women—has been utilized as a means of influencing her to yield implicit obedience to her mankind, whether he be father, brother, or husband. She has made him, in a certain sense, her god, and in yielding all to him she has ceased to think in the terms of her own individuality, accepting the common opinion that the Eastern woman lives for her home and the amusement and the material comfort of her husband. A mental deficiency bill was passed upon her centuries ago, and the laws command her husband to keep her under restraint. Her menfolks expect her to be deficient, and have carefully guarded her from opportunities of becoming otherwise. Her husband has not associated her with any of his outside life, and she has found little or nothing in his conversation to stimulate or to broaden her mind. Considering her as a being who only understands her children and the petty gossip of the women's quarters, he has deprived her of the mental possibilities which have reached the men of the East. He has not only tried to teach her not to think for herself, but the Eastern masculine has endeavoured to make her understand that she cannot think. Nor is this tendency entirely abolished by modern education. The young girl fresh from her school in Cairo or Calcutta, where she has caught glimpses of a new world, and where her brain has been slightly awakened, marries and goes into the traditional home, where her faith in herself is gradually diminished by living constantly in the atmosphere of ignorance and superstition which still rules so largely in her woman's world. Finally, she gives up trying, resigning herself to the standard of the man-made world in which she finds herself, and her husband becomes her keeper in every sense of the word.

The Eastern woman naturally tends in this way to lose her self-reliance, which she is not allowed to exercise. She often decides few matters for herself, even the small details of her daily life being settled by her husband. The effect is insidious, but none the less relaxing, since the faculty of responsibility, like every other faculty, is strengthened only by exercise, and passes away with disuse.

Can the woman of the East be awakened to an advanced development without harm to herself? Within her is found an enormous amount of suppressed capacity for good and evil. This suppression, which has been her cue for generations, possesses great dynamic power. Force becomes dangerous when confined; it should be directed, and unless properly guided and controlled, when it does burst forth, as it is bound to do with these women who are becoming educated and learning their power, it is likely to riot widely, with havoc for its effect. The Eastern woman who has traded upon her emotional nature for her livelihood, who has used these same emotions to keep her husband in a land where divorce is easy and where polygamy is practised by many, may be guided by her feelings rather than her intellect, using her new-found freedom to bring her lasting unhappiness instead of the joy which she now believes is lying just outside her doors. In India advance has come too rapidly at times, and the woman in her desire to slavishly imitate her sisters from the West has shocked the conservative traditions of her nation, and thereby greatly retarded her cause. The Egyptian woman when in England or France becomes almost ludicrous in her attempts to be like the European woman, forgetting that she lacks the foundation of the years of freedom and equality with men which bring judgment and confidence to the woman of the Western world.

The woman of the Orient is awakening and is setting herself the task to consider what is best to be done. How can she remedy the deficiency of the social life of her land? The case is not a hopeless one by any means, even though her capacities and wonderful possibilities have lain dormant for so long. Many of these women now see the things that are wrong; they see the iniquity of a system in which they are not allowed to choose their own mate; they see the crying wrongs of their antiquated marriage and divorce laws, made for another period than the twentieth century—laws which do not fit the present conditions, however successful they may have been in other times. These women are learning to respect themselves and their position, learning to appreciate and value the weight of their majorities, and some are having the courage to speak out. These bolder ones are being punished for their intrepidity; but it does not check them. The cause for which they are working is gradually becoming more and more possible with the advent of education and Western influences, which are causing the present-day educated men of the Orient to require a certain amount of education in their wives and daughters. As this new order comes to the land of the Nile and the Ganges, the old-time woman who passed her days lounging on the divans, eating sweets, drinking coffee, and gossiping with servants and friends as ignorant as herself, will pass away. The new woman of the East will never be a suffragette; she will never attend mass meetings nor carry banners marked "Votes for Women"; indeed, it would be as incongruous to think of these sheltered women doing such a thing as to imagine the long row of mummies at the Museum of Cairo suddenly starting a procession down the aisles of the museum. These women, however, are setting up a high standard for themselves, eager to accept all the Western world has to offer them by way of education and growth, while they feel that they have the capacity to attain the objects of their new ambitions.

In all this change, will the Oriental woman remain the same as regards the deepest things in her nature? Will she keep her innate sense of modesty, her womanliness, her love of home and children, her feminine qualities which seem to us of the Western world almost a weakness, but which comprise her appealing charm? We cannot but feel that although the woman of the East may change radically in the outward expression of her life, inwardly she will remain the same. Indeed, it would be a great mistake if the Eastern woman became satisfied with any mere superficial imitation of her Western sisters. She would lose her birthright. She would lose the consummate opportunity of being an Oriental in an Oriental world, and bringing out of her treasure things new and old for the benefit of the women of every race. Her message to the world of the West in the devotion and the keeping of the home, in the love and pride of children, in her self-effacement for the good of the family, is a high message and in no period has it been more insistently needed. It is this contribution which the woman of the Orient will bring in return for the education and enlightenment from the Occident.

If the Western woman comes to the Oriental bringing in her hands the fair gifts of intellectual advancement and broadened life, her Eastern sister will not be her debtor if she, by example, presents in return the even more precious charms of obedience, modesty, and loyalty which fundamentally are the priceless jewels in the crown of the world's womanhood.

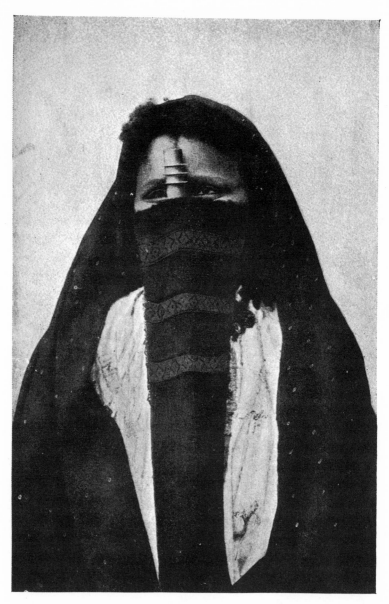

EGYPTIAN WOMAN OF THE LOWER CLASS.

To face p. 19.

The Harim and the Purdah

CHAPTER I

EGYPTIAN WOMEN OF THE PAST

THE word Egypt opens the Book of Romance to the traveller in the East, and he longs to come under the spell of its mysterious grandeur, and gaze upon the monuments which will speak to him of the power and splendour of a people long since gathered to their gods. It is a land in which to dream dreams and see visions. The temples, broken columns, and great pylons call with a voice that must be heard even by the prosaic tourist, and the hands he sees painted upon the walls of Denderah or Deir-el Bahari will beckon him when sitting in office, club, or home, far from the dazzling sands or burning sun of Africa.

The charm of the land of the Pharaohs is very real, and it is hard to speak of Egyptian life in a calm and lucid style, or free oneself from extravagant descriptions.

Egypt and its fascination are favourite themes

for novelists and writers of travel, and yet in spite of a good deal of general knowledge we remain curiously ignorant of the Egyptian woman, from the point of view of her moral and mental development.   In common with women of other Oriental lands, she has been an object of mystery to the Western world.   We know that in the olden time, in the days of the Pharaohs, she held an important place in the life of her world.   We see her pictures on the tombs, temples were erected in her honour, and we know that there were queens who in their day governed their country with dignity and rare ability.

In former days the purity of the blood of the royal line was assured by the marriage of a brother and sister, the queen reigning equally with the king.   If a queen of royal birth took as her consort a male not descended directly from a royal mother, even though his father might have been a Pharaoh, at the death of his wife he was compelled to abdicate in favour of the son or daughter who could call the queen " mother." This was shown when Thotmes I was compelled to resign his crown in favour of that great Queen Hatshepsu, his daughter, who for twenty years governed Egypt.   Although her reign was a stormy one because of her half-brothers who claimed the throne, her name and features erased from all the monuments, and omitted from the official tablets and chronological records, yet enough was left to show that her power had

RAMESES AND HIS WIFE.

To face p. 20.

been great and that she commanded the attention
of the world.   It is said that Hatshepsu had herself everywhere depicted as a man, wearing the
dress and even the beard of the stronger sex,
perhaps hoping in this way to gain a greater
allegiance of her people.

One of the most interesting temples along the
Nile is that of the first woman ruler of Egypt
of whom we have accurate knowledge.   One rides
over the hot sands beneath a burning sun to a
series of great terraces and broken white columns
against a background of tiger-coloured preci-
pices.   This beautiful temple of the XVIIIth
Dynasty, called by the Egyptians " the Sublime
of the Sublime," was dedicated to Amen Ra and
his companion gods, Hathor and Anubis, but
it was really erected to commemorate the glorious
reign of a great queen.

Another woman who influenced Egypt was the
mother of Amenophis IV, the great reformer.
He disestablished the State religion, some say
at the instance of his mother; confiscated the
lands and destroyed the power of the priests
of Amon who were becoming all-powerful; and
established the worship of one God.

Solomon evidently held the Egyptians in high
favour.   He had many wives before he married
a princess of Egypt, but we hear of no palaces
being built especially for any of them, nor of the
worship of their gods being introduced into
Jerusalem.   Yet we are told that a magnificent
palace was built for Pharaoh's daughter and that

she was permitted, although contrary to the laws of Israel, to worship the gods of her country.

Then there was Hypatia, an Alexandrine, who established a school of philosophy where learned men from all parts of the world came to listen to her words of wisdom ; and in the British Museum there is a manuscript of the Old and New Testament, written on parchment immediately after the Council of Nice, by an Egyptian woman, which goes to prove that men did not possess all the knowledge nor learning of their time.

We all know the story of Cleopatra and the part she played in the downfall of her country, and history abounds with tales narrating the bravery, courage, and charm of Egyptian women.

Women are also associated with the religion of this old land. The worship of Isis was as general as the worship of her brother Osiris, and this goddess is reverenced as the representation of true and loyal wifehood.

Another woman, Athor, the goddess of love, who was called the " Great Mother " and served as the protectress of earthly mothers, was good and beautiful, lovely and gentle, the goddess of love and joy. Neith was worshipped as the goddess of art and learning. Maat was the goddess of truth and justice ; and in ancient times judges, when trying cases, held a small figure of the goddess Maat in their hands, and touched the persons acquitted with it, to show that they had won their cause.

There was Taur, the goddess of evil, and Sekhet, typical of the scorching, destructive power of the sun, and many minor goddesses whose emblems, seen on columns and walls of the ancient ruins, tell us that in those days woman was thought fit to represent Divinity.

The women of ancient Egypt were evidently not secluded, as is shown by the story of Pharaoh's daughter who was going with her train of maids to bathe when she found Moses. The story of Potiphar's wife and Joseph would never have been told in modern times, as a man-servant would not have dared to go to the women's quarters.

This valley of the Nile has always been the home of mystery and charm. The inscriptions on its tombs and temples have been deciphered and receive much attention in modern days ; but they are not more interesting than is the woman of Egypt, who, as we have learned, enjoyed greater liberties and received more honour than is the heritage of her modern daughters. It is difficult to understand her, as even yet she represents traditions and the habits of dead centuries, fit to be relegated to the past.

She is the Sphinx of this Oriental land, and will not easily give to the world her secrets.

THE MOHAMMEDAN WOMAN.

When first one visits Egypt, romance seems to peer from beneath the veil of each black-robed figure, and mystery lurks behind the intricate carving that covers the windows where one is sure some languid beauty sits waiting for the moment when her lord and master will be gone, that she may wave a white hand to the passionate suitor below. This idea of Egypt is generally derived from highly coloured and erotic novels which always make this country alluring and often sensual. To one who has been given this highly seasoned food for his imagination to feed upon the modern Egypt, with its great glaring hotels, its motor-cars, its shops that might be in London or New York, is a great disappointment.

Illusions will again be lost if one is permitted to enter the beautiful homes on the fashionable drives of Cairo, for they are not Eastern in any sense, nor is there anything about them to indicate that their owners are Orientals. They express no individuality, and might belong to any person of means whether in the East or the West. The drawing-rooms are furnished in French fashion, with gilded chairs, a grand piano, hangings and curtains made in England or France. Great glass chandeliers holding the glaring electric lights express the cosmopolitanism which the mistress feels she must show the world, in order that she may not be considered as belonging to the old school of Egyptian womanhood.

One hears the word harim and instantly conjures up an Arabian Nights picture of rare hangings, subdued lights, beautiful odalisques

lounging on soft divans, slaves, incense, and a
general air of sensuousness pervading the entire
place.   I read a book not long ago written by
a well-known woman writer who says, " I am
thankful to say that I have never been within
a harim except twice, and the memory of that
dreadful place will rest with me for many years."
Yet she admits that on her first visit to this
" dreadful place " she had no interpreter and
could only draw upon her imagination to give
the women she saw their position in the elaborate
household.   This imagination was evidently a
vivid one, as she believed that many women she
saw were " the poor deluded slaves " of the
master of the house, while quite likely they were
the innumerable relatives and woman-servants
that always throng the rich man's home.

In reality, in present-day modern Cairo, if
one enters the harim of the better class, or of
the official class, one is greeted by a hostess
dressed in the latest French creation, tea is served,
while the politics of the world are discussed easily
in either French or English by the polished, up-
to-date Egyptian women.

The word harim is much misunderstood
by the people of the Western world.   The Arabic
word harim simply means the women's
quarters.   The selam-lik are the apartments
in which the men of the household have their business offices, receive their friends, and pass their
time, while the harim-lik are the apartments
reserved for the female members and children

of the family. The literal meaning is exclusive-
ness, seclusion, privacy. In its restricted sense
it embodies the two meanings of the women
of the household and their exclusive apartments.
In the wider acceptance of the term we understand by harim an established social system
deriving its sanction from a body of laws pro-
mulgated by the Arabian prophet Mohammed.
When a woman is harim it means that she is
secluded, and we hear the expression in regard
to schoolgirls. "Yes, my daughters go to
school," a mother will say, "but they are
kept harim."

In Persia and Turkey the word zenana is
used, and in India the common form of expression for the woman who is not seen by any male
except those of her immediate family is, "She is
purdah-nashim, or simply purdah." The purdah is the screen that shuts her from the outside
world, and the Oriental, whatever his race,
whether in Egypt, Turkey, or India, whether he
calls it the harim, purdah, or zenana, speaks
of it in his literature and poetry as the
"Sanctuary of Conjugal Happiness."

One can live years in the East and get little
idea of the life of the Moslem woman of the
better class. In Egypt ten million out of the
twelve million inhabitants are followers of the
prophet Mohammed, and to understand at all
the Eastern woman one must learn something
of the religion that dominates the entire life of
the Mohammedan. The actions of the Moslem

woman, whether in India, Arabia, Egypt, Persia, or Algiers, are controlled and forced to comply with the laws made by the Arabian prophet of the seventh century, and even to-day his word practically governs each act of the domestic life as well as the world outside the home.

Before Mohammed's time there were no social, religious, nor educational institutions in Arabia, as we understand them. Unlimited polygamy, slavery, drunkenness, polytheism, gambling, child murder, and plunder existed. He taught that there was but one God, forbade child murder, limited the number of wives to four, forbade the use of intoxicating liquors, gambling, usury, and gave women a definite legal status.

The reforms inaugurated by this wonderful man effected vast and marked improvement in the position of the women of the Eastern world. Her status had degenerated from that held in ancient times until her position was extremely degraded. She was the chattel of her father, brother, or husband, like his camel or his sheep, and could be bought and sold as any other chattel. She was an integral part of her husband's estate and was inherited by his heirs. The son inherited his father's wives and often married them. This Mohammed severely censured, and laid down most exacting laws in regard to the women lawful for a man to marry. He says :—

And marry not them whom your fathers have married ; for this is a shame and hateful, and an evil way—though what is past may be allowed. Forbidden to you are your mothers and your daughters, and your sisters, and your aunts, both on your father's and your mother's side, and your foster-mothers and your foster-sisters, and the mothers of your wives, and your stepdaughters who are your wards, born of your wives, and the wives of your sons, and ye may not have two sisters.

He is severely criticized that he authorized polygamy, but when one remembers the wild, lawless people whom he governed, it seems that he showed extreme moderation in limiting the number of wives to four. He added that a man might possess the slaves within the household, and his followers say he was compelled to put in this postscript in order to quiet the unrest that was caused by the new domestic regulation which was so contrary to all ideas then controlling his immediate world.

He expressly stated that if a man could not deal justly and love equally all his wives, he must then marry but one. All true believers quote this as meaning that Mohammed really intended his people to be monogamous, as it was fully known that no man could love four women with equal ardour. The husband is also enjoined to partition his time equally amongst his families, and there is a saying that if a man inclines particuarly to one of the women of his household, in the day of judgment he will incline to one side by being a paralytic.

He allowed women to inherit property, although he gave a girl only half the inheritance of a boy. A wife may inherit one-fourth of her husband's estate if there are no children, and one-eighth if there are children; if there is more than one wife, the eighth is divided equally amongst them. A man may inherit one-half of his wife's property in the event of her being childless, but only one-quarter if she leaves children, and neither one can disinherit the other.

Yet the laws show clearly that a woman was not legally the equal of a man, as it takes the testimony of two women to equal that of one man, and the price of a woman's life was only fifty camels instead of the hundred camels demanded for the life of a man. There is a reason for this other than the mere disregard of women. Those days were lawless days, when tribe was fighting tribe and the non-fighting women were naturally not held in such esteem as were the men who were needed to fight in the continuous tribal wars.

Moslems claim that the Mohammedan woman is more truly protected by the laws of Mohammed than are the women of Western countries. She can dispose of any property that she may receive, either from her family or her husband, as she sees fit. She is not responsible for the debts of her husband; she can sue and be sued; or she can make contracts or enter into any business undertaking without consulting her husband; and she may even take him before the courts if he does not live up to an agreement he may have made with her.

Yet this wily Eastern prophet did not believe in the absolute equality of women ; as he says :—

Men are superior to women on account of the qualities with which God hath gifted one above the other, and on account of the outlay they make from their substance for them ;

and he warns his followers from making too large settlements on them or in giving them too many valuable gifts :

And entrust not to the incapable the substance which God hath placed with you for their support ; but maintain them therewith, and clothe them, and speak to them with kindly speech.

A Moslem woman is supposed to share the responsibilities of life as well as its pleasures. In the case of destitute parents, sons are required to contribute two-thirds towards their support, while the daughters must add their third. This is a very wise law, because Egypt, like practically all Oriental countries, makes no provision from its public funds for the maintenance of the poor or old. Each family must care for its own helpless.

Many reasons are given for the laws compelling the women of Mohammedan lands to be veiled and to pass their life within the inner apartments reserved for their especial use. Some say that Mohammed caused women to be veiled because of his jealousy of his young wife Ayesha ; others claim that the prophet, becoming enamoured by the beauty of his adopted son's

wife, caused her to be divorced, afterwards
marrying her, contrary to the laws he himself
had made ; he wished to protect men from being
subjected to the temptation which had overtaken
him and had brought upon him the displeasure
of his people. But the seclusion of women was
found in Asia, in ancient Rome, in Syria, and
even in Athens, long before the time of
Mohammed. It was in practice amongst many
Oriental nations from the earliest times, and
quite likely Mohammed simply adopted the customs of the people with whom he came in
contact on his conquering tours.

The seclusion of women, especially among the
nomads, can be traced to the warlike habits of
the people. In times of war the enemy would
first of all carry away the women, children, and
cattle of the tribe with whom they were fighting. In order to protect the helpless they were
kept in inner rooms. The richer and stronger
the family, the more secluded were the women,
and it became a mark of caste to be kept within
the women's quarters, or protected. Thus what
first originated as a necessity became afterwards
a matter of aristocracy, and the man who could
keep his women strictly harim was looked
upon as higher in the social scale than one who
was compelled, from economic reasons or otherwise, to allow the females of his household to
come and go freely in the world.

An Egyptian woman, from the time when she
is seven or eight years old, never shows her face

unveiled to any man except her father, her brother, or her husband. No chance is given the followers of the Arabian prophet to have the little flirtations that are so dear to the heart of many of her Western sisters. Mohammed says :—

And speak to the believing women that they refrain their eyes and display not their ornaments, except those which are external; and that they throw their veils over their bosoms, and display not their ornaments except to their husbands, or their fathers, or their husbands' fathers, or their sons, or their husbands' sons, or their brothers or their brothers' sons, or their sisters' sons, or their women, or their slaves or their children. And let them not strike their feet together so as to discover their hidden ornaments.

The present-day Mohammedan woman observes this law more strictly than was at first intended, even to not being seen by the father of her husband. I know an Egyptian woman who is never seen by her father-in-law except on the first day of the year, when he calls upon her to wish her the joys of the coming year. She enters the room closely veiled and offers him the season's greetings, then leaves without further conversation. I was calling upon an Indian Mohammedan woman who could not enter the room until her father-in-law had left it, as it would have been a serious breach of etiquette for him to see her.

This seclusion does not rest heavily upon the Mohammedan woman, as she considers it the desire of her husband to protect her, and she would be the first to resent the breaking of her seclusion, as showing that she had lost value in his eyes. She lives for no one except her family, is supposed to be of no interest to any one else, it being a great breach of social decorum for any male member of a family to even inquire about her. A man would never say to another man, " Is your wife well? " He would say, " Is your household well? " And the husband would never speak of his " wife " to another man, but would speak of his " house," which would naturally include the female occupants.

The harim is the " Holy of Holies " in the Moslem world. Even a police official would hardly dare to penetrate the women's quarters in search of a criminal. When a man has retired to his harim he is free from any disturbing influence from the outside world. If a friend or enemy should call and servants would say that the master was in the harim, the caller would be compelled to leave or wait until the master was disposed to enter again the selam-lik, or rooms assigned to the male members of the household.

The greatest evil in the harim life lies in the dreadful seclusion and the paralysing monotony. Many of the older women are unable to read and write, and they pass their days in weary idleness and a vacuous routine which is only broken by visits to women friends as mentally impoverished as themselves. Not being allowed the friendship of the opposite sex, they are denied the stimulation of the mind which would no doubt result from the interchange of ideas with men who come in contact with the outside world. Naturally the intellectual development is restricted, and this starving of the mentality of the women must have a result detrimental to the rising generation.

Seclusion also makes a woman very much more the actual possession of her husband than she would be if allowed to come and go in the world, to know her rights and the means by which to enforce them. Although the laws are very much in her favour, in regard to property rights especially, it takes a woman of more than ordinary courage and intelligence to break away from the walls which encircle her and parade her troubles in open court. We are told of the wonderful laws allowing the woman to dispose of her property as she wishes; but we are not told that she may give this property to her husband, and when once within the harim, pressure is often brought compelling the woman to give all that she possesses to her husband, making her doubly helpless and wholly within his power.

They have a proverb that a woman must always answer the call of her husband, " even if she is at the oven." Her happiness depends entirely upon the treatment she receives from him. His visits to the harim are the only breaks in the monotony of her life, and he brings to her the only touch she may have with the great man-world outside. By a few men the wives are treated as if they were intellectual equals, but these are few and far between. The average Oriental treats his womenfolk as if they, were upon a lower plane than himself, " brought up amongst ornaments and contentious without cause."

One would judge that, handicapped as they are, Moslem women would take no part in the political or social life of their country, but facts prove that they can rise to great heights and exhibit rare courage and executive powers in time of need. Ayesha, the favourite wife of Mohammed, showed an instance of bravery and courage that might belong to women of any land. When Ali, the cousin of the prophet, rebelled against the successors of Mohammed, Ayesha took the field against him, commanding the troops in person at the " Battle of the Camel," and in later days they have shown that the restrictions of the harim do not deaden the fires that burn in women's breasts when tyranny or oppression rules their land.

In Persia, where Mohammedanism in its strictest sect has sway, the women have been known to rise in force and demand the rights of their people when all the efforts of the men have failed. In 1861, at the time of the great famine, foodstuffs rose to an exorbitant price, because of a few greedy officials who were enriching themselves at the expense of their starving countrymen. It was impossible to bring the matter before the Shah by the methods

generally employed, but the women rose, and
one day thousands of them surrounded his
carriage as he was returning from a hunting
trip, and stating the wrongs of his people, demanded that he should make an investigation.
The Shah was thoroughly frightened at the sight
of this unprecedented exhibition on the part of
his usually unseen subjects, and promised all
they asked, and, what was more wonderful, kept
his promise. The leaders of the party who were
causing the distress were beheaded, and the price
of bread was diminished by half within twelve
hours. It is only a few years ago that the
women of Persia confronted the President of
the Assembly in his hall, and tearing aside their
veils and producing revolvers, confessed their
decision to kill their husbands and sons and add
their own dead bodies to the sacrifice if the
deputies should waver in their duties to uphold
the liberties of the Persian people.

These Moslem women display a fortitude and
courage that is almost fanatical in times of
persecution. Thousands in Persia have given
their lives for their faith in Baha Ullah, the
leader of a sect of reformed Mohammedans.
They have been dragged from the harims to the
public market-places, where they have been subjected to unheard of indignities before having
the privilege of dying for their faith. They have
also been compelled to sit in rows facing the
public execution grounds while their husbands
and sons were beheaded before their eys, but

A WATER-CARRIÈR.

To face p. 36.

even the torture and death of those they loved did not cause them to waver from what they believed to be right. The story of one woman exemplifies the fanatical courage that will dominate such a shut-in woman, when in some dim, tragic hour she has been compelled to give her contribution in the life she loved to her religious cause. In Tabriz one day a crowd of women were seated facing the executioner's block, and amongst them a delicate, dainty woman who had been protected all her life within the harim of one of the prominent men of Tabriz, but whose death had left his women helpless to bear the brunt of his enemy's wrath. Chance had made this enemy the city Governor, and he remembered that the family of the man he hated even in death were followers of Baha Ullah. On this morning in June the mother was brought to see the death of her fourteen-year-old son, her only child. When the executioner had done his work, the head was tossed into her lap, and she was told " Take back your son." She stood up, and holding the loved head in her hands, held it towards the sky, as if to give it as an offering to the God who seemed to have deserted her in her hour of need, looked long into the closing eyes, then threw it to the official's feet, saying, " I do not take back what I give my God ! " and turning quickly, took her place among the sorrow-maddened women.

Her cousin, who told me the story and who was a witness to the scene, said to me : " It is impossible for a Western woman to understand a Moslem woman. Perhaps because of our exclusion and the lack of means of self-expression, we have over-developed our inner emotional natures, which at times of sorrow burst forth like a hidden flame. We not only gave our lives in those dread days of Tabriz, but what is worse, we gave the lives of those we loved—and still lived on."

The women of Egypt have as yet had no reason to rise up *en masse* and show what they may do in times of national distress. It is unusual for the women of any Mohammedan land to usurp the prerogatives of men. They are fundamentally intensely feminine, the home their only domain. Sa'adi, the Persian poet, said :—

No happiness comes to the house of him whose hen hath crowed like a cock.

It will be many years before the Egyptian woman joins the ranks of the militant suffragettes, and tries to blow up the Pyramids or deface the walls of Egypt's famous temples in the spirit of emulation and zeal for *the Cause*.

CHAPTER II

THE MODERN EGYPTIAN WOMAN

THE conservative woman of Egypt prides herself that she never leaves her home. I know several ladies well advanced in years who say they have never been outside their homes since they were brought there as brides. An Eastern household is composed of many people, and this seclusion of the women does not cause such loneliness as would be felt by a Western woman if thus closely confined always to the home. In the East the patriarchal life prevails, and the financially fortunate member of the family finds himself supporting an immense army of poor relations, who act in all capacities, from maids in the kitchen to the servants at the door. They expect little or nothing as wages, but they *do* expect that the prosperous member of their clan or family will provide clothing, food, and a roof beneath which they may live.

In all Egyptian homes of the better class there are many servants. They are not the competent, trained servants to which we are accustomed, and it takes many of them to accomplish what one well-trained servant will do in England or America. They have no system, each servant doing his task in his own appointed time and in his own way. Within the harim the servants are generally women, and they are on much more familiar terms with the inmates than are servants in the West. They take on a feeling of equality with their mistresses, taking part in the conversation when guests are present, entering doors without knocking, and generally considering themselves as part of the family. Mohammed taught that all true believers are free and equal—the servant the equal of his master.   This is one of the reasons that the traveller is often surprised by having the donkey-boy offer his hand when saying good-bye.   He does not intend it as an impertinence ; he simply wishes to bid his patron " God speed " in the Western manner.

The women of the harims take much time to dress, and spend long hours in the public baths, if they do not possess that luxury at home. They take great care of their skin, using all the arts to keep it soft and unwrinkled. They have not yet learned the charm of beautiful hands, and the manicurist has not yet penetrated the harim, but it is only a question of time when she will arrive, as the Egyptian woman seizes with avidity every means of improving her personal appearance.

Many of them tint their straight black locks

with henna, by making a paste which is allowed
to dry on the hair for twenty-four hours, then
removed.   This, when used not too freely, gives
a charming glint of reddish gold to the thick
hair, and utterly obliterates any trace of age.
The henna-tinted locks are not seen as much
as formerly, as the custom is passing out with
the advent of the newer generation, and is mainly
to be seen on the older women or the women of
the desert.   In former times the nails of the
hands were tinted a deep orange, but this also
is being relegated to the " things that were," as
the young girls are beginning to see that instead
of a beautifier, it makes the hands appear most
untidy.   I have seen an old lady with her fingers
stained a deep brownish yellow to the first joint,
the palms of her hands, the toes, and even the
bottoms of the feet coloured with the henna
paste.

The house dress of the Egyptian woman is
a long *négligé* made in an empire form
or what we used to call a " Mother Hubbard,"
with the fullness of the cloth gathered to
a much-trimmed yoke, and ending in a
train that sweeps the floor.   The wearer may
follow her fancy in the choice of goods with
which these dresses are made.   The ordinary
dress worn every day is of some material easily
laundered, but the gown for gala occasions is
often most elaborate, made of rich silks, satins,
or brocades with great figures in gold or silver.
Many of them appear as if made of cloth origin-

ally intended for furniture covering. If she has
a wide range from which to select the material
for her dresses, she also is not restricted in the
choice of colours, as each woman indulges in
whatever shades she most admires, and a party
of women with their red, blue, yellow, and mauve
creations look like a party of animated dolls
dressed for a fancy bazaar.

The hair is braided in one or two braids and
allowed to hang down the back, sometimes tied
with strings on which dangle gold coins or balls.
A veil is always worn over the head, hanging
down to the waist line. It is very graceful and
adds to the dignity of the Egyptian woman.
With the poor this head covering is a large piece
of cotton with a gay-coloured border, and even
ladies wear in the morning a cotton veil, but on
dress occasions it is of chiffon or net elaborately
bordered with gold or silver, or in some cases
sewn with sequins, very similar to the shawls
offered by the vendors in front of the big hotels.

The feet are slipped into toe slippers that can
easily be removed when entering the living-rooms
or when sitting upon the divans. In the matter
of footwear there is a wide range from which
to choose. From the wooden bath clog to the
tiny heelless covering for the toes, embroidered
in gold or silver or even tiny seed pearls, the
Egyptian woman's slipper is a thing of beauty
and dainty femininity. Stockings are considered
a superfluity while in the house, except by those
influenced by the customs of foreign lands.

If the lady wishes to make a call she dons a black silk or satin skirt with a long train, and over it ties a piece of black goods shaped like a large apron hanging down the back instead of the front. The lower end is brought up over the head and tied under the chin, acting as hat and shoulder covering, completely disguising the form. Over the face below the eyes is tied a piece of white chiffon. This is really an addition to the woman's charming appearance, as the present-day Egyptian woman is wearing the veil so thin that the shape of the features can be dimly seen, softened and refined by the delicate chiffon, until even a plain woman takes on an appearance of beauty that perhaps vanishes when the veil is removed. She is allowed to show her chief attraction, her great black eyes, which peer at one curiously over the folds of white. They are not so large as are the Indian woman's eyes, but they are very expressive, shaded by long straight lashes, which are generally touched up by kohl, since even with the advent of modernism the Egyptian woman cannot be persuaded to relegate her kohl-pot to the lumber-room.

The woman of the labouring class, seen on the street, is dressed in a long gown hanging straight from the shoulders, over which, when she leaves her home, she drapes a large black shawl covering her from head to feet. The veil of this class of woman is of black cloth, so thick that it is impossible to distinguish the features beneath it, and often weighted at the bottom with

gold or silver coins. Covering the nose is the
disfiguring piece of wood which holds the veil
in place. The picture of this sombre-clad woman,
with her ugly veil and grotesque nosepiece, is
taken by the average tourist as representing the
Egyptian woman, while, in fact, she represents
only the lower class, such as the wife of the
labourer, the small artisan, or the petty merchant.
These women may be seen on the streets walking
with the stately grace that is given to the woman
who carries a burden on the head, or five or
six of them may be seen sitting on a flat-bottomed
cart drawn by a much decorated donkey *en route*
to visit relatives or watch the festivities connected
with a marriage, or going to the cemeteries. This
last seems to be a favourite excuse for an outing
with women of this class, as it gives them a
chance to have a good gossip on the way, and
opportunity of strolling in the open air, which
must be a great boon to the poor in the large
cities, as their homes are small, dark, dirty, and
most unsanitary. Yet as one lives in the Orient
and sees the conditions under which the great
majority of the population live, one grows to
believe that there are no such things as microbes,
else all these people would have been dead long
ago.

Even in modern Cairo one rarely sees a lady
except as she passes in a closed carriage or
limousine. Women do not go to the mosques,
as Mohammed said that women in places of
public worship distracted men from the real busi-

THE TAILOR.

To face p. 44.

ness which brought them there. They are also never found in restaurants, hotels, nor coffee-houses. In fact, an Egyptian woman never goes to a place where she might be looked upon by men other than those of her immediate family. Even the most modern product of the present system of education would hardly dare to be seen in any place that was not harim. At the bazaars held for charity and other public functions a day is set apart when the women may visit them without danger of being looked upon by men. An Egyptian woman told me that these men must be educated and elevated before Egyptian women will dare to go freely upon the street. Even a foreign woman dreads passing the outdoor cafés, where the men turn noisily in their chairs and stare rudely at the woman who has the courage to pass them. In the case of an Egyptian lady, I was told that these men do not confine their rudeness to stares, but that the low remarks made to her confirm the belief that the time is not yet ripe for the Egyptian woman to try to enter the world, so long closed to her.

These harim women are just beginning to learn the joys of shopping. Formerly the husbands or fathers bought the goods for their dresses, or the shopkeepers sent their assistants, who laid the gay stuffs and jewels on mats within the courtyards, where the women could make their choice. But now in some of the larger shops parties of veiled ladies may be seen fingering the soft silks and satins, looking with curious

eyes at the hats, and selecting the jewels with
which they love to adorn themselves.   Cairo is
the happy hunting ground of the Parisian
jeweller, as Egyptian women are noted for their
love of bracelets, earrings, necklaces, and pins.
The old-time heavy gold chains and hoops are
losing their charm, and now the lady whose
husband has a purse easy to open buys long
pendant earrings set with many diamonds, bracelets of pearls and rubies, rings of turquoise and
sapphires, and necklaces of emeralds.   Quantity,
not quality, she desires, and the colour and purity
of a stone are not so much to be desired as the
size or number.   The women who make no claim
to modernism are still seen in the goldsmiths'
shops in the native streets, sitting in front of
the tiny cupboard-like holes in the wall, weighing, pricing, trying on the great barbaric hoops
of gold for the ears, or the chains with large
hammered pendants, made in the same form and
with the same design as those worn by their
mothers and their grandmothers.   The merchant
does not need to originate new designs to attract
the conservative Egyptian woman who still clings
to her native jewelry.   It has been the same
shape and design from time immemorial.

Another product of the West has penetrated
the harims of Cairo—the French dressmakers.
Many of the rich merchants' wives and the wives
of the officials who cannot get their gowns direct
from Paris, and who are discarding the straight
empire pattern for clothes more *à la mode*, get

their dresses fashioned by these clever French women, who come to the women's courtyards loaded down with fashion books, tape measures, and a running stream of flattering talk, leaving with many orders written in their little books. It must be admitted that the Egyptian woman looks best when dressed in her native costume, which mercifully disguises the over-abundant flesh with which most women who spend their lives within the harims are blessed. Sweets, a sedentary life, and many sweetened drinks conspire to make the lady of Egypt extremely fat, after the first flush of youth is past. This is not a sorrow to her as it would be to her Western sister, and when she has arrived at the age of thirty, and the pounds that she feels should come with the advancing years have not been added to her figure, she sends to the chemist for a mixture to convert her into the present ideal of Egyptian beauty. This ideal in the olden time, if we may judge of the pictures seen upon the walls of the tombs and temples, was that of a slight, willowy figure. But that ideal has changed. The woman now seems to strive to be as wide as she is long, and because of this fact and also because stays are not looked upon with joy by the Egyptian woman, who has always been allowed an uncompressed figure, the modern dress is not adapted to her style of beauty.

Women are not prisoners in any sense of the word, nor are they pining behind their latticed windows as we are sometimes led to believe by writers of fiction. They visit freely amongst each other, and their visits are not confined to the passing of a few senseless platitudes that generally mark conversation of Western women making afternoon calls upon each other. They do not "call," they go for a visit of several hours or even days.

When a lady enters the home of her friend, she takes off the veil and the cape-like covering of her head, steps out of the long black skirt, and stands arrayed like Solomon in all his glory. They dress as elaborately for their women friends as if to meet admirers of the opposite sex, and they spend hours drinking the delicious coffee, sipping sherbets, eating fruits or confectionery, and chatting over the gossip of the day. When time for serving the meal arrives, a large tray is brought into the room and placed upon a low stand, around which the women group themselves in comfortable attitudes on rugs. From these trays they help themselves to the deliciously cooked mutton or chicken, the vegetables and deserts with which it is laden. Pork is never served, as it was forbidden by Mohammed. They eat with their fingers, using only the right hand, as the left hand is ceremonially unclean, and after the meal a servant pours water over their hands from a long-spouted brass ewer, the water falling into a brass basin. Many of the ladies smoke, but it is not a universal habit. If they indulge in the habit with which we always associate the Eastern woman, it is by using a large water-pipe with an extraordinarily long, supple stem, the smoke passing through perfumed water and becoming cool before reaching the user's lips.

The Eastern woman loves perfumes and prefers them much stronger than we of the Western world think agreeable. A hostess will pass around the little wooden scent-bottles, and each guest may add as much as she wishes to her already over-perfumed body. The mixture is not always pleasant to sensitive nostrils. Incense and sweet smelling woods are often burned in little braziers and add to the congeries of odours.

Many of the old-time Egyptian women cannot read; indeed, it is stated that only three out of a thousand women could read ten years ago; their conversation is therefore confined to the gossip of the neighbourhood: who is married, who is engaged; the social and financial standing of the families involved; the presents and the trousseaux. Society is divided into cliques, as in any other part of the world, and there is a decided " Who's Who," especially in Cairo and in the larger towns.

The woman's life seems to centre around her children, since it is this evidence of Allah's blessing that makes her greatest happiness. A great part of their talk is involved in the discussion of their children's ailments, the remedies, their children's education and life in general. There are no nurseries in Egypt, and both boys and girls live within the harim until they are seven years old, when the boy, if he does not go to

4

school, has a tutor and lives in the selam:-lik.
.When, as at present, Government schools are
established in every small town and village in
Egypt, both boys and girls go to school. The
girl is kept strictly harim even in the school,
and the teachers are women, who guard carefully
from men's eyes the girls who are entrusted to
them for the day.

Besides visiting with their friends or relatives,
the Egyptian women go to weddings, where they
look upon the dancing and hear the singing from
their places behind the screens, or they make
pilgrimages to the tombs of saints or holy men,
where they pray for the health of their children;
or, if they have not been so fortunate as to have
children, they pray for that blessing. They do
not pray *to* the saints, as even Mohammed
himself cannot answer prayers, but they believe
that the austere lives passed by these holy men
will intercede for them with the Great and One
God.

An Egyptian friend of mine, telling me of the
efficacy of one of the places of pilgrimage in
the cure of eye troubles, said :—

"Yes, I believe in these charms obtained at
the tomb of some of the marabouts, and I have
been on several pilgrimages, although it is not
much encouraged in our family. You saw my
brother's wife to-day. She has visited the tomb
of every saint in the vicinity of Cairo, but it
is just because she is restless and wants to get
out. She cares no more about the saints than

you do, but it gives her an opportunity to get away from my mother. My life, that you think so restricted, is wildly exciting to what it was when I was a girl at home. Mother is most conservative, and will not even allow a man-servant near the harim. Her cook has never seen her, although he has been in the family since I was a baby. Here in the country I have men-servants who see me unveiled, but they are the descendants of slaves who were in the family of my husband for generations, and that is per-mitted if we are not too orthodox."

I noticed while visiting friends in the country with this progressive, educated Egyptian woman that if we passed an ordinary fellah, or workman, she did not take care to cover her face. If we met an overseer or a man above the farmer class, she very carefully drew her veil across her face, leaving only the eyes visible.

The women are very superstitious, and believe in the efficacy of charms and amulets for every known disease. Nearly every woman wears around her neck, lost to sight amidst the innumer-able chains with which she covers the upper part of her body, an amulet or charm of some kind. Perhaps it is a silver box containing a few words of the Koran, or a small piece of parchment with mystic letters written on it, guaranteed to guard her household from harm. All Egyptian women know of charms and lotions and shrines or mystic words to give the wife who has not presented a son unto her lord. One of the first

questions asked by Egyptian women is, " How
many children have you? " If the answer is
" None ! " they cannot keep the looks of pity
from their eyes, nor the sympathetic words of
condolence from their lips. They are also most
generous in giving talismans to remedy this de-
fect, and will wax enthusiastic over the beneficial
effects of some favourite pilgrimage, amulet, or
prayer.

I have a piece of sheepskin with the ninety-
nine names of Allah written upon it in gold,
intended to insure, not only the advent of a son,
but also, if bound upon his arm, to guard him
from all danger throughout his lifetime.

At the opera in cosmopolitan Cairo one may
hear rustlings and low laughter from behind the
closely screened boxes, and know that an
Egyptian Bey or wealthy merchant is there
with his family, allowing them to enjoy the play
and watch the people in the house, themselves
unseen. But this joy is given usually only to
the women of Cairo, as the smaller towns have
not as yet become sufficiently modernized that
the women may go to the public theatres. In
the conservative homes, if a hostess wishes to
entertain her guests with professionals, she sends
for the singing girls or dancing women to come
to her home, and there they perform before the
ladies, who watch them from the divans, and talk
and laugh with their entertainers, getting far more
amusement from them than by simply looking
at them on the stage.

Fortune-tellers are often brought into the women's quarters, and blind men who chant the words of their sacred book, the Koran. This latter is a popular form of entertainment, and even to Western ears the sad, minor music has a charm, although after a time it becomes monotonous to one who cannot understand the Arabic in which the Koran is written.

Even the conservative Egyptian mother is now beginning to see that she must educate her daughter as well as her son, if she wishes her to make a good marriage. The modern Egyptian youth does not care for an ignorant wife who can only entertain him with household gossip when he comes from office or shop.

There is ample opportunity given the Egyptian girl to obtain an education, as the Government has established schools in every city, town, and village. One sees also a great number of private schools for girls, supervised by every imaginable type of mistress. The Italian, Spanish, French, and English woman is taking advantage of this craving on the part of young Egypt for education. Many of these schoolmistresses are unfitted for their work, but as yet her pupils are not able to judge of the quality of information they are so eagerly absorbing. The mission schools, next to those provided by the Government, are perhaps the best equipped with trained teachers from England and America. These latter schools are filled with bright-faced young

girls, who are taking the newer ideas to their
secluded mothers, who shake their heads dole-
fully over the new spirit of independence so
swiftly creeping into the lives of their children,
and which they fear, but to which they must
accede.

Egypt, in common with the entire world, is
experiencing vital changes, and her younger
women, although walled in by custom, tradition,
and habit, are eager to get into step with their advancing sons and husbands. It is only the older
woman who is the implacable foe of progress,
as she fears a change may mean the destruction of her little world. Yet she is fast losing
the power as well as the wish to resist it, and
the number of schools for girls shows that a
real awakening to Egypt's greatest need is being
felt and met. At first the mother feared her
daughter would be led astray from the true Faith,
but the English Government bore this well in
mind when establishing the educational system.
The Koran and the practical observances of its
tenets are taught by faithful followers of the
prophet in the schools, and this has induced
mothers to look with complacent eyes upon the
new learning.

Infinitely better daughters and prospective
mothers come each year from the Government
and mission schools, if for no other reason than
that they are intelligently trained in domestic
economy and in the laws of hygiene. The frightful waste of infant life which heretofore has been

caused by the ignorance of mothers will stop. The present training of the young girl strikes directly at this huge infant mortality and in the coming mother, educated and equipped for her duties, lies the hope of Egypt.

CHAPTER III

MARRIAGE, DIVORCE, POLYGAMY

SOCIAL LIFE OF EGYPTIAN WOMEN

THE Koran enjoins marriage on all and calls bachelors the worst of mankind. Consequently there are few spinsters or bachelors in any Moslem land, and a woman who is divorced or widowed must have another husband found for her as soon as possible.

Although Mohammed believed that all men should be married, there were four classes of women against whom he warned his fellows :—

A *Yearner*—that is, a woman who has children by a former husband and wishes to get everything possible for them from her present husband.

A *Deplorer.*—One who is constantly deploring the loss of her first husband and stating his virtues to the disparagement of the present incumbent.

A *Backbiter.*—One who is kind to her husband's face and behind his back accuses him of cruelty, miserliness, and ill-treatment.

A *Toadstool.*—A beauty who is lazy and tyran-

nical and uses all the substance of her husband
to buy silks, jewels, and perfumes with which
to adorn herself.

There is no courtship as we know it. The
marriage is made by the parents or by a "go-
between," and the parties most interested do not
see each other until the night of the marriage,
although they may have exchanged photographs
and have heard eulogistic descriptions of each
other. But there are no shy meetings, no
gazing into the eyes of the loved one. A
girl would be considered as lacking in modesty
and maidenly reserve if it were known that she
attempted to see the man to whom she will be
compelled to owe all allegiance and who will
practically own her, body and soul, as soon as
she is his wife.

During the time before the marriage the
bridegroom, if a man of wealth, sends his bride-
to-be many costly presents, generally in the shape
of jewelry, silks, fans, slippers, and boxes of
sweets. Her gifts to him are cigarette cases,
embroidered sleeping suits, a rich fez, or some
other practical evidence of her affection.

In families of any social pretensions what-
soever, there is drawn a marriage contract which
stipulates the amount of dowry and whatever
business relationships are entered into by the
husband and wife. If the amount of dowry is
not expressly stated in the contract, the woman
is entitled to the customary dower of a woman
of her class, which is judged according to that

received by the other female members of her family. This contract can also contain a stipulation that the husband may not marry another wife so long as the present wife is living with him, and it also often states that the wife may divorce her husband for certain expressly stated causes.

There are two kinds of dower, one called " prompt " which is all paid at the time of the marriage, the other where only part is given at that time and the rest retained to be paid in case of divorce or on the death of the husband. In the latter case the dower must be paid before the other debts of the estate are settled. The wife has absolute rights over her dower and can refuse to go to her husband's home until it is paid.

The trousseau is provided by the father of the bride, and the articles she takes to her new home in the shape of furniture, jewelry, etc., are her property and can be taken with her if she should return to her father's home or if she should be left a widow. The bridegroom is supposed to help pay the expenses of the elaborate feasting which lasts from three to seven days, and which is often a great drain upon the resources of both families. Custom has commanded that no parsimony shall be shown at this time of rejoicing, and each family tries to outdo its neighbour in the form of entertainment offered to its guests.

Theatrical entertainments are held in the courtyards, or in the large guest-room. Dancing

girls dance and jugglers perform, while food is
most plentifully provided, but there is no drinking
of intoxicating liquors in the home of a follower
of Mohammed. In the place of wines, sherbets,
fruit juices, and coffee are served.

The culmination of the festivities comes when
the bride in a gaily decorated carriage is conducted to her new home. In the streets of any
large city one often sees these processions, the
band leading the march, dozens of singers preceding the carriage, and friends following, all
trying to show their joy in the happy event.

According to Western ideals there is one great
bar to the lasting happiness of the Moslem
woman, and that is the question of divorce. It
is said that 90 per cent. of the marriages in
Egypt end in divorce, and that two people who
live to an old age together without one of them
being divorced are rarely found. Mohammed
has been severely censured because of this great
blot upon the progressive laws he made for his
people, but before his time there was no check
on divorce ; a man could divorce often and for
no reason, and a woman was helpless. This
wise man laid down laws far in advance of his
time on this subject, and (what was then an unheard of thing) allowed a woman to divorce her
husband for explicitly stated causes.

If they divorce for mutual incompatibility—that
is, if they both agree to it—there need be no
question of the courts ; but if the wife wishes
to be free and the husband will not permit it,

the woman may go before a judge and state her case, and if her charges are proven she will be granted her petition. Often a woman will return her dower or agree to forfeit the part not yet paid, or in many cases make a money payment to the avaricious husband in return for her liberty. A case not long ago came before the judge where the husband treated his wife brutally in order to force from her a certain sum of money in exchange for her freedom. The woman paid the sum demanded, then took the case before the judge, and proved that his cruel treatment would entitle her to a divorce, and the courts compelled the man to return the money to his ex-wife with an added gift.

The different sects have different modes of procedure. One requires the husband to pronounce the words of divorce once in a single sentence and not live with his wife for three months, when the divorce is accomplished. Another form requires that the words be pronounced three times in succession at the interval of a month, the divorce becoming effective when the last formula is pronounced. Another formula allows the husband to say three times in succession, " I divorce thee ! I divorce thee ! I divorce thee ! " and the legal separation takes place.

A woman may say to her husband, " Give me a divorce in exchange for my dower," and if the man will say, " I do," a lawful dissolution of the marriage is effected.

Whatever the rule, divorce is very easy for the Moslem husband, and the woman lives in constant fear that she will hear the words " I am discharged from the marriage between you and me," and will be compelled to return to her home. This insecurity of the marriage bond causes the woman to hoard what money she may obtain, and takes away the interest she might otherwise have in the affairs of her husband, fearing that prosperity may only mean that he will yearn for a younger and more beautiful woman to share with him his riches. It also makes her try in every way to preserve her beauty, buying cosmetics and talismans that clever merchants assure her will aid in retaining the love of her husband.

In the event of divorce the woman is commanded to remain single three months, but the man may marry immediately. There is no especial disgrace attached to divorce, yet the woman's value is lowered to a certain extent, and quite likely she will not be able to make so good a marriage again.

No child under two years may be taken away from the mother, as the Koran commands her to suckle the infant for that period. Unless it is proved that she is totally unworthy to bring up her child, or unless she marries an unbeliever, the boy is entitled to live with his mother until he is seven years old, and the girl until she is nine, when the father takes the guardianship of them both. Often they are allowed to live on indefinitely with the mother, especially the girl, if the father marries again and the new wife does not wish the care of the children of her predecessor. This makes the burden of divorce fall heavily upon the innocent children, as the mother generally marries and her husband may not care for the children of another man ; consequently they are left in the care of the mother's parents or other relatives, who quite likely consider them a superfluous addition to an already overcrowded household, although the father is compelled to contribute towards their support.

If divorce is prevalent in the Land of the Nile, that other great domestic evil, polygamy, is slowly dying out, mainly for an economic reason. All the wives in a family are supposed to have equal support, and in these days, when the women of Egypt are beginning to know and crave the luxuries of life, it is hard for a man, unless of the very wealthy class, to provide for more than one family. In a rich household each wife would demand, not only her own suite of rooms, but quite likely her own house and staff of servants, and she would see that her husband did not show favouritism in regard to clothes, jewelry, or amusements towards the women and children in his harim. Often in poorer homes one sees two wives living in peace together, but the man with more than one wife is becoming rarer each year. It is said that not one man in fifty has more than one wife. The cynics say that it is because divorce is so much easier and cheaper, but we believe that it is because of the higher ideals that are coming to the Egyptian along with the education that he is receiving from the Western world.

It is easy for the Western mind to take exaggerated views of the unhappiness of the life in the harim. I found, among the better classes, with whom I came into contact more than I did with the very poor, the same average of happiness that prevails in any land. Seclusion which seems so dreadful in our eyes has grown to be a matter of caste, and the older women, at least, have no desire to depart from it. The power of the husband is greater than it is in foreign lands, but he is generally a kindly man who leaves the women's department strictly alone, to be ordered as his wife desires. It is she who has charge of the children while in infancy, teaching them or having them taught the Koran, taking them with her on visits to friends, and being with them much more than does the average Western mother of the same class. A middle-class Egyptian woman does practically the same things as does the wife of a middle-class Englishman. She cooks, washes, mends the clothing, keeps the house, and sews her children's dresses. If she is able to have servants—and one is very poor in Egypt not to be able to afford at least one servant—the work of the household is superintended directly by the mistress. Of course she may not go to the market nor to the shops, but she inspects the food when brought to the house by the vendor or the cook.

The care of the clothing is a great task if there are many sons in the family who dress in the native costume, which is made of light-coloured silk ; the long black cloak is prone to sweep up the dust of the streets. The children of the poor wear only a short shirt until they are about six years old, but the children of the rich don European dress, either made in the house or bought in the shops. The ready-made clothing has found its way to the harims and saves the mother much work, as the sewing-machine is not so well known there as it is in the homes of the West.

Although the Egyptian woman is not seen in the mosques, she is very religious, and more zealous in the faith than is her husband, who has a chance to broaden his religious views by coming in contact with people of other beliefs. The wife does not observe the prayers as strictly as does her husband, but she has been taught her Koran in childhood and follows its precepts to the best of her ability.

The woman, like women all over the world, is much more rigidly ruled by her superstitious beliefs than is the man. She attributes the extraordinary phenomena of Nature to the work of good or evil spirits and believes in placating them or controlling them as far as possible. These evil spirits are liable to lurk in all places, in the ovens, the wells, and even in the market basket, which is covered to protect it from the evil eye of covetous passers-by, or to guard

A WOMAN OF THE MASSES.

To face p. 64.

it from a wandering spirit who may be seeking a place of retreat.

The women in general are very ignorant in regard to all sanitary laws, and there is an enormous amount of preventable sickness within the harims. Children are allowed to eat what and whenever they wish, and sweets are indulged in at all times. All babies suffer from eye trouble, mainly caused by uncleanliness. A baby is not washed for eight days after birth, then if the father or mother is suffering from any form of skin disease, it is considered fatal to put water on the child. Flies and mosquitoes abound, carrying contagion to all. Doctors are unknown amongst the poorer class, and the mothers are in the hands of unskilled midwives at the time of child-bearing, and the mortality is great.

When the angel of death enters the household of an Egyptian, it may be known by the wailing of the women. The custom of weeping and wailing, beating of the breasts, and tearing out of the hair still prevails on the death of the member of a family. The body is buried within twenty-four hours. It is enclosed in a coffin which is covered by a rich shawl or piece of embroidery and carried to the cemetery on the shoulders of men, preceded by blind men chanting the Koran and followed by friends and relatives. The same ceremony is observed for the women as for the men.

The soul is supposed not to leave the body for three days. The first night an angel whispers

5

in the ear of the deceased, " What is your faith? " and the soul must answer, " I am a Moslem." The angel again whispers, " In whom do you believe? " and the soul will answer, " I believe in the One God," and the third question is, " And who is your prophet? " and the answer, " Mohammed is the Prophet of God," allows the soul to be left in peace.

Three days, seven days, and forty days after death memorials are held at the home of the late deceased, when friends call and offer their sympathy, and food and money are distributed in great quantities to the beggars. At times of festivity or mourning the poor come in crowds, and are never turned away empty-handed. There are practically no almshouses in Egypt, nor any organized charity, but Mohammedans are commanded to give one-twentieth of their income to the poor. Whether they follow this law exactly or not, they are very generous to those in need, not giving with much discernment, but always willing to drop a coin into the outstretched hand or to fill the empty bowl.

One cannot judge of the life of the average Egyptian woman by living only in Cairo, where the note of modernism has sounded with such call as to reach even the inner rooms of the harim, but in the smaller towns of Egypt one sees the real Egyptian life, untouched by the customs of alien lands.

I visited in a home on the banks of the Nile and watched with interested eyes the life around

CHILDREN ON THE NILE.

To face p. 66.

me : saw the mother attend to her household
duties in the morning, giving the servants directions for the day's work, measuring and weighing
out the stores to the cook, and taking his accounts
as he came from the market-place with the day's
provisions.   An old blind woman came in the
morning to give the children their lesson in the
Koran.   She would start a surah, then the
children would repeat the remaining verses in
a sing-song voice, the slightest break in the
intonation calling forth a rebuke from the leader,
whose nodding head kept time to the chant.   At
nine o'clock the older children took their books
under their arms and started for the village
school, in the same noisy manner as do our
children at home.   I watched the fellaheen as
they lifted the water from the river to irrigate
the thirsty fields, and saw the black-robed
women filling their water-jars and placing them
upon their heads with a beautiful sweeping ges-
ture, walk gracefully away to their little mud
huts that could scarcely be distinguished from
the sands around them.

Trains of camels passed our wall on their way
to the distant city, and the shepherd boys drove
their flocks of sheep and goats in search of
pasture.   I remembered Browning's beautiful
David, who sang :—

And I first played the tune all our sheep know, as one after
      one
So docile they come to the pen door till folding is done.

They are white and untorn by bushes, for lo, they have fed
Where the long grasses stifle the water within the stream's
   bed.
And now one after one seeks its lodging, as star follows star
Into eve and the blue far above us—so blue and so far.

We watched the little boys ride the great un-
wieldy water buffaloes to the water side, slipping
off their backs to allow them, groaning with
content, to wallow in the sluggish waters, and
when the hard white stars came out in the
sapphire sky, we looked far over the Libyan hills,
which had changed from the gold and opal of
sunset to the grey blue that heralds the coming
of the Egyptian night.   The evening breeze that
always comes with the setting of the sun brought
the smell of the dese.t to us, and the deep swish
of the Nile came as an accompaniment to the
cry of the muezzin from the tiny mosque in the
distance, and we saw its response in the fellah
kneeling beside his waiting camel, lifting his
hands to the heavens, as the clear, bell-like voice
came over the evening air :—

There is no God but God, and Mohammed is His Prophet.

BEDOUIN WOMEN IN FRONT OF TENT.

To face p. 69.

CHAPTER IV

THE WOMAN OF THE DESERT

" BEHOLD the townsman," cried one of the Bedouins, " they have for the desert but a single word, while we have a legion."

The desert, which in many eyes is a wilderness of desolation, has for the dweller beneath the tents another aspect. It is the desert which he loves, where he was born, under the brown tents of his tribe where he hopes to pass his life, and in the sands where he wishes to be buried. He loves each one of its many phases, from the sand burnt to powder by the white fire of the noonday sun, to the cool breeze of the dying day, that causes the smoke from the many fires to rise in blue-grey wreaths to the evening sky, which changes from violet to greyer blue, and then to the intense dark blue of the precious sapphire.

The Bedouin, to whatever tribe he may belong, sitting astride his camel, padding softly through the desert sands, sees before him the low black tents of a desert village, and knows that he may descend and find a welcome. The host will say

to him, " Every stranger is an invited guest,
and the guest while in the tent is the lord
thereof." He may sit before the large round
bowl of mutton and eat his fill, and when the
stars have come out, and seem so near that
he may put up his hand and pluck them
from their field of blue, he will be conducted
to the guest-tent or to the tent of the headman,
and, wrapping himself more tightly in his long
cloak, he will lie down secure, knowing that
his life is safe so long as he remains a guest of
the tribe, having eaten of their salt and drank
their water.

These Arabs of the desert are proud with a
pride we do not understand. They are proud
of their long lineage, of the purity of their blood,
of their unbroken traditions. They are an
impulsive, restless people, who, with their emotional temperament, give impetuosity to everything which they touch. They are the real
adventurers of the world, and their nervous, high-
strung, daring characteristics have become so
absorbed into their very being as to have become
permanent marks of their race. At the seat
of all troubles, in countries where the Bedouins
are strong, one finds them ready to do and dare
anything that appeals to their imagination. At
the rising of a Mahdi, it is the Arab of the desert
who is his strongest support, who will die for
him, who will sweep down like a holocaust upon
the people who do not share with him his beliefs
in the cause, for which he throws his life away

with a bravado that makes men of a more sluggish
blood gasp in astonishment.   This cause must
appeal to his emotions—those same riotous
emotions which never produce, but always ruin.
We are told that the Bedouin is the author of
complete desolation, and that destruction follows
in his pathway ; that his effects are always
sinister, and that this race brings ruin to any
land where they have been permitted to have
full sway.   We know he is not a creature of habit,
and that routine, a settled existence, a fixed round
of duties, are things which he does not understand
nor practise.   He does not reason and is not
practical, yet it is the Arab that has succeeded
in sending the faith of El Islam around the
world, and every movement of revival comes
directly from the desert.

Few people travelling in Egypt or Algeria see
the real dweller beneath the tents.   There are
Bedouins in the cities, and one soon learns to tell
them, with their keen eyes, their eager faces,
and majestic stride, from the more placid, self-
satisfied Egyptian.   But in the city he is not
his true self, as life in the cities has a permanent
and degrading effect on the character and
physique of the race ; the fire of the desert dies
within him.   It is in the shifting sands beneath
the tents that he is at his best.   There he carries
out his tribal customs, and there he practises
that wonderful virtue of hospitality that
Mohammed, himself an Arab, laid upon his
people.   He said, " Whoever believes in God

and the Resurrection must respect his guest ;
and the time of his being kind to him is one day
and night ; and the period of entertaining him
is three days ; and after that if he does it longer,
it benefits him more, but it is not right for a
guest to stay in the house of a host so long as
to incommode him." It is said that even a
deadly enemy may come to the tent and demand
water and salt, and it will be given him, and
he will be allowed to rest for the night.   In
the morning he will be sent on his way, and his
life is safe until he has passed the boundary of
the tribe's dominions, then his enemy is entitled
to follow him and kill him if he can.

All tourists passing through Egypt look
forward to a few days passed in the desert. The
guide paints in glowing colours the wonders of
the sands, the colours of the evening sky, the
sounds of the hobbled camels as they wait for
the morrow's march, and the traveller from the
West decides to see for once the life of which
he had read and dreamed so many years.   In
every soul is a cry for romance, a desire to leave
the prosaic everyday life which he knows too
well, and explore the mysteries of the unknown,
hoping that there by chance he will find food
to feed his hungry imagination. A trip to the
desert does this for many people.   There the
broker or the banker, with the wife he has looked
upon for many years, sit in front of their hired
tent, and watch the camel man, as with scolding
voice he prepares the growling, surly camels for

the night.   When all is quiet but the distant
barking of the dogs, they sit in front of the evening fire and watch the stars come out in the
sky that seems a great inverted cup of blue
above them.   The camel drivers, dragomen, and
guards sprawl in easy attitudes and chant mournful, weird songs that have come to them from
the Persian mystics of olden time.   These people
from New York or London do not realize that
they are not seeing the real desert nor the people
of the desert.   The setting is all staged most
carefully by the wily dragoman, who imports his
Bedouins from the neighbouring villages, who
dresses tents until they would cause the man who
calls them home to stare in blank amazement
at their tawdry hangings.   The only thing he
cannot import is the wonderful dessert sands, the
sky, the cooling breezes that always come when
the sun has set.   These are free for all, to the
ragged camel driver as well as to the man who
scatters so freely the English gold.

We had the pleasure of knowing the chief
of a large tribe of Bedouins, and from his castle
on the edge of the desert were permitted to make
many visits to these picturesque people.   Our
first glimpse of the true man of the desert was
obtained from the visitors in the guest-house,
where any Bedouin could stop from one to three
days as the guest of the chief, and every day
about sundown strange white-robed men with
guns strapped across their back rode up on
horses and dismounted at the gate, craving the

hospitality of the chief.   There were always from
ten to thirty guests within the rest-house, men
looking like the Senouisses, who cause so much
trouble for the unbelievers of foreign lands.   We
were told that many of them were going to join
their brothers in Tripoli to fight against the hated
unbeliever.   They were not permitted by the
Government to go openly, as Egypt was supposed
to be neutral, so they took the long caravan
journey of thirty days across the desert to aid
in what they considered an unjust war against
the true faith.

Within the harim of my hostess were rooms
set aside for travelling Bedouin women, but they
were seldom occupied, as the women of the tents
are not wanderers like their husbands, unless the
whole tribe moves.   My hostess was a young,
educated girl, to whom the confines of a Bedouin
harim must have been very wearying.   The laws
concerning the women of the tribe were very
strict, one being that a woman must stay within
her apartment until the birth of her first child.
My friend was not blessed with children, but
had been compelled to conform to the usages
of her husband's family, in part at least, by
remaining within her home for a year.   Now she
went about freely among the villages of the
Bedouins near the castle, only taking the precaution of being veiled.   These Bedouin women
were quite another type from those seen in the
cities.   They had magnificent physiques, tall and
supple, and carried themselves with a stately

grace. They were dressed in long, straight,
cotton gowns of blue or black, and a many-
coloured sash was wrapped around the waist.
The only foot covering was the anklets of silver
that fell down over the instep ; and they wore
over their hair, which was braided in many
braids, and in which was plaited small gold coins
that clinked as they moved their heads, a veil
of black with a coloured border, or of dark red
with a yellow border. This veil adds to the
dignity and beauty of a woman in a most
charming manner. At the time of feasting or of
gaiety the plain veil is changed for one sewed
with bright-coloured beads or sequins.

From the lower lip to the neck, and lost in
the covering of the dress, are three dark blue
lines of tattooing. This is seen now only on
the older women, and is being thrown on the
altar of modernity by the daughters of the
Bedouins who have peeped into the world and
are trying to be like their more sophisticated
Egyptian neighbours. The hair is straight and
black, and with many has been given a tinge
of red by washing it in henna. I saw no grey-
haired women ; because those who have been
touched by the finger of time, kindly custom
has allowed to dye their locks, and there were
many flaming heads above wrinkled faces.
While a guest with the Bedouins, they were quite
determined to give me the touch of red that
to them is so beautiful. They say it keeps the
hair cool and prevents it from falling out,

protecting it from the burning sun. I resisted,
although I watched the process, which was most
interesting. The henna powder is mixed with
water until the consistency of a paste, and then
the head is covered and left for the night, when
in the morning it is washed, and if not applied
too thickly there is just a glint in the dark locks.
Henna is also applied to the nails of the fingers
and toes, and with many it practically covers the
fingers to the first joint, making the hands look
most uncleanly to European eyes. The inside
of the feet and the palms are not forgotten by
the Bedouin or the Egyptian woman who has
conserved the customs of her mother, but the
henna-dyed hands are rarely seen now by the
newer generation, who have relegated the henna-
pot to the lumber-room along with the tattooing-
ink. A great mass of jewellery was worn, not the
diamonds and rubies found in the French shops
of Cairo, but the true ornaments of a barbaric
people. Great hoops of gold were in the ears,
one from the top of the ear, another hanging
from the lobe. The neck, even to the waist-line,
was covered with chains formed of balls of gold
or of coins, and on the arms were bracelets. In
writing coldly of the Bedouin woman, her tattooing, her henna-coloured hair, her kohl-blackened
eyes, and her massive chains of gold and anklets
of silver, it seems as if she were living in an
age of barbarism, yet it is becoming to her
rich colouring, and she is not over-dressed.
They all belong to the time and place, and

are made for these women, who need strong
settings for their savage beauty.

The women of the desert are much more free
to come and go than are the women of the cities,
and it is only when they come in close proximity
to an Egyptian village that the Bedouin expects
his wife to be secluded. They do not mix with
members of the other sex as do the women of
the West, because that is contrary to the instincts
of all Eastern women, but naturally they cannot
be confined so strictly within the tents as can the
women who live in houses. In each tent is a
division or curtain, behind which the women retire
when men approach, but they may be seen sitting
in front of their doorways, and passing to and
fro in the villages without veiling their faces.
They pass their spare time when not occupied
in the household duties in weaving gaily coloured
blankets, striped red and yellow and black.
These constitute the woman's fortune. My
friend took me to one tent in which there were
forty of these blankets piled around the edge of
the tent, and she said, " Five or six of these in
the possession of a woman and she is considered
rich in this world's goods. This woman is a
multi-millionaire." She was an old woman who
seemed to be the leader of her village. It was
she who met us and conducted us to the guest-
tent, which was at least twenty by thirty feet
in circumference, and which was hung with these
beautiful hand-woven blankets. The sands were
covered with rugs on which we sat, and on which

the large round tray was placed for the meal which the kindly hospitable women insisted that we should eat with them.   There are no tables, beds, nor chairs.   The Bedouin says that we can never understand the desert until we get close to her, rest our feet on her sands, and our head on her bosom—

> But man is earth's uncomfortable guest
> Until she takes him on her lap to rest.

One thinks of a tent in the desert under the pitiless sun as a most uncomfortable place of retreat, but I found it quite the opposite, as the strong wind, that seems to be always trying to temper the actions of its enemy, blew over the desert and entered the open flaps, and crept under the turned-up edges of the tent, fanning into flame the fire of sweet-smelling woods that had been kindled in the tiny brass jar.   Water was hanging in porous bottles and in sheepskins in the draught, and when mixed with the perfumed syrups was cool and refreshing.   Coffee with a touch of ambergris in the cup was served, and melons were given us in great cool slices.   These latter are a favourite fruit of the desert people, I presume because of the vast amount of water of which they are composed, and water is the luxury of all luxuries to those who dwell among the sands.   An old Arabian poet said : " There are seven things when collected together in a drinking-room, it is not reasonable to stay away.

A melon, honey, roast meat, a young girl, wax lights, a singer, and wine." Twice during our visit was perfume sprinkled over us, and the brass brazier was often replenished with sandal-wood, a small packet of the latter being given us as we were leaving. The Arabs, in fact all Eastern people, love perfumes, and they use them in far greater quantity and of stronger essence than we consider delicate. Musk and a heavy perfume distilled from jasmine and roses seems to be a favourite. Mohammed himself loved perfumes, and speaks of them in his promises to the faithful who shall fall in battle : " And the wounds of him who shall fall in battle shall on the day of judgment be resplendent with vermilion and odorous as musk." We visited the smaller tents, and in some it was impossible to stand erect even at the ridge pole. In one was a young baby wrapped in white cloth and twined with yards and yards of camel's-hair rope, only his tiny head and feet protruding to show that there was a real baby in the bundle. He was bound practically the same as are the babies of our North American Indian. I took him in my arms, and he stared at me with great black eyes, and then he laughed and cooed, much to the delight of the young father, who stood proudly by. The mother was quite a young girl, not more than fifteen years old, I should judge, and in her shyness she retired into the security of the tent, resisting all my friendly overtures to have her picture taken with the baby in her arms. Children abounded; there will be no race extinction of the Bedouins so long as they remain in their deserts. Their little brown bodies snuggled up to us, and their black eyes twinkled saucily as they shyly held out their hands for the gifts which evidently my friend always brought with her. They were a much better type of children than are those in Egyptian villages—strong, pretty bodies, and without the unhealthy eyes that are seen so much on the young in Egypt.

In every tent was hung a gun, as robbers are frequent visitors, and each dweller in the tent must protect his own. He keeps a fierce and noisy dog that sees a stranger far across the sands, and one is followed far beyond village confines by these canine police.

Polygamy is practised by the Bedouin more than it is by his city brothers. I visited in the tent of a woman who was the second wife of her husband, the other wife living in a tent adjoining. She had two children, and the first wife one, and from what I heard there was not the most pleasant relationship between them. Divorce is also one of the evils, and these primitive men take advantage of it to an alarming degree. Nearly every one I met had been divorced some time or other. It was such a common occurrence that it produced no feeling of shame in the woman who had been divorced.

The Bedouins are so proud of their lineage that they wish to keep the tribal blood pure, and it leads to intermarriage.   Cousins are frequently married, and often a whole tribe is related in some manner.   I was told that the Bedouin settled an argument with a scolding or recalcitrant wife by giving her a good chastising with a stick.   While in Cairo I met a most charming Bedouin who had left the sands for the gaieties of the city.   He was quite the polished gentleman to be found in any city, and I was surprised when told that he had divorced his Bedouin wife because she was not as progressive as his cosmopolitanism now required, and my gossipy friend informed me, " They used to quarrel dreadfully and he would beat her most frightfully."   I saw the lady in question, who had returned to the tribe and remarried, and I rather admired the hardihood of the somewhat effeminate man who would dare to try to beat this great stalwart Bedouin woman, who looked as if she would take an active part in any chastening that might be passing around her tent.

There is no such word as " privacy " in the Bedouin vocabulary ; their private life must be an open book to all the tribe.   Their one great blessing is the wonderfully clear, dry air, which gives them health and vigour and makes them immune to many of the diseases that afflict their Egyptian neighbour.   But if they leave the desert and go to live within the cities, they fall easy victims to the great white plague, tuberculosis.

The Bedouins are followers of Mohammed, but

6

they put their faith in holy tombs and charms and sacred groves. They are not so strict in regard to prayers as are the people who live within call of the muezzin, and the religion of the women seems to be more superstition than worship of a God. They placate a God who may do them harm, and they have innumerable charms and amulets for the guarding of their children. In the desert whirlwinds they see sweeping across their sands are " ginns " and evil monsters ; and at night, when a star shoots across the dark blue sky, they believe it is a dart thrown by God at an evil genie, and they whisper, " May God transfix the enemy of the faith." Around the naked children's neck is hung a small box containing some quotation from the Koran that will guard them from the evil eye, that curse most dreaded by all mothers of an Eastern land. For every evil that man is heir to, the Koran is the cure. A few words from its precious pages are bound upon the arm of the camel driver, who feels that with this as guardian he will not be lost upon the trackless sands. When ill, the wife will call the astrologer, who writes a few words upon a piece of paper, and soaking it in water, gives it to the wailing child, and the mother is assured that all will soon be well, because has he not drunk of the very fount of wisdom, the words that came from God?

The old custom of a life for a life prevails in the desert, and feuds are handed down from father to son. If a father or brother is killed, it is the duty of the son or brother to take the life of the enemy of his house. In the olden time there was blood money which could be paid, although it was considered a cowardly thing to accept it. A man's life was worth a hundred camels, a woman's only fifty, but the man of honour asked the life. The chief of the tribe has the power to decide in all cases between his people, and the English Government does not materially interfere in the life of the Bedouin.

In regard to the custom of taking a life for a life, there is a story told of how in the early days the missions made a convert from Mohammedanism, the only convert made among these tribes. In a blood feud a man stabbed his enemy, but not fatally, and fleeing to the tent of a friend he lingered there many days. This tent was one visited by the missionary of the Christian faith, and while lying on his bed of pain the wounded man heard of a faith that said, " Love your enemies," and before his death he sent word to his tribe that they must forget his death and not try to avenge it. He even sent word that he forgave his enemy. This was so astonishing that neither could the man who killed him nor his tribe believe the fact, and secretly the enemy decided to find for himself what had caused the unheard-of message to be brought to his tent. He learned of the new religion that said, " Revenge is Mine, saith the Lord," and he became the only Bedouin convert to the Christian faith.

Living in this home on the edge of the desert we saw the real life of the tent people. We watched them as, weary and tired looking, they returned from their long journeys. We saw the trains of laden camels as they started for the distant cities. We saw the shepherd boys drive in the flocks of sheep or goats, looking as they did in olden Bible times.

CHAPTER V

INDIAN SOCIAL LIFE

THERE is no woman in the world who is so bound down by custom, so tied to the wheel of conventionality, as is the Indian woman, both Hindu and Mohammedan. In the olden times the ancient law-makers realized the danger menacing a people surrounded by an inferior race, as were the natives of India compared to their Aryan invaders, and instituted that remarkable social system that peculiarly affects the women of the country, and is the cause of many of the evils that has made her life one not to be envied—caste.

Hindu society is divided into hundreds of communities consisting of several clans, each clan having its own peculiar customs and iron-bound rules. The clans are composed of families, governed by the family custom, which in turn must obey the clan custom, and these must be governed by the rules of the community. If a person violates the custom, he forfeits all the privileges which he or his family may have in the life of the community. His social life is entirely cut off from other families and from the protection of his people. No one of his community will eat or drink with him, visit his house, or marry his children. The priest will not serve him, the barber will not shave him, nor the washman wash for him. He will be absolutely alone and friendless in the world, not able to get employment, even allowed to starve by the members of his own family, who dare not help him, knowing they themselves would be outcasted. He may not have the solace of joining another caste, either lower or higher, because he must live and die in the caste in which he was born.

Originally there were only four great castes in India : the Brahmans, or priestly class, who held all the intellectual or cultural prerogatives ; the Kashatriyas, or warrior caste ; the Vaisayas, or merchant caste ; and the Sudras, or working class. Below that still are the outcastes, who are almost slaves, and do the lowest menial services. Manu, the great law-maker, said that the Brahman issued from the head of Brahma, hence his intellectual superiority ; the warrior from his arms, the husbandman from his thighs, and the Sudras from his feet, thus exactly placing the man's social position in life.

The laws of caste as explained by Mr. Dutt, a Hindu writer, are as follows—

Individuals cannot be married who do not belong to the same caste.

A man may not eat with another not of his own caste.

His meals must be cooked by persons either of his own caste or by Brahmans.

No man of an inferior caste is to touch his food or the dishes in which they are served, or even to enter his cook-room.

No water or other liquid contaminated by the touch of a person of inferior caste can be made use of—rivers, tanks, and other large sheets of water being held incapable of defilement.

Articles of dry food, such as rice, wheat, etc., do not become impure by passing through the hands of a person of inferior caste so long as they remain dry, but cannot be taken if they become wet or greased.

Certain prohibited articles, such as cow's flesh, pork, fowls, etc., are not to be eaten.

The ocean and other boundaries of India must not be crossed.

These rules would not be so oppressive if there were only the four original great castes into which society was first divided, but now each class is divided into thousands of sub-divisions, whose members may not intermarry, nor eat together, nor even touch the food prepared by those of another community. Mr. Sidney Low has very well expressed the difficulties caused by this very intricate social ruling in his " Vision of India "—

" To get a loose analogy, we might suppose that everybody who could claim descent from one of the old Norman families in England formed one caste ; that members of the ' learned pro-

fessions,' who had never soiled themselves with
commerce, were combined in a second ; and that
others consisted exclusively of bankers or money-
lenders, or of pork butchers, costermongers,
bricklayers, and so on *ad infinitum.*

" Add that a man born in the costermonger
class would remain, or ought to remain, a
member of that connection to the end of
his days, and that he would, bring up his
sons to the same business ; that a green-
grocer ought not to eat food in company
with a poulterer, that a baker might not give his
daughter in marriage to a cheesemonger, and
that neither could have any matrimonial relations
with a bootmaker ; and, further, that none of
these persons could place himself in personal
contact with a clergyman or a solicitor—imagine
all this, and you begin to acquire some faint
notion of the involved tangle in which the entire
Hindu community has managed to get itself
enwound."

Mr. Low quotes from the census report of
Sir H. Risley further to illustrate what the caste
system means in the matrimonial sphere, that
sphere that especially touches the womanhood of
India—

" He imagines the great tribe of the Smiths
throughout Great Britain bound together in a
community, and recognizing as their cardinal
doctrine that a Smith must always marry a Smith,
and could by no possibility marry a Brown, a
Jones, or a Robinson. This seems fairly simple ;

there would be quite enough Miss Smiths to go round. But, then, note that the Smith horde would be broken up into smaller clans, each fiercely endogamous. Brewing Smiths," Sir H. Risley asks us to observe, " must not mate with baking Smiths ; shooting Smiths and hunting Smiths, temperance Smiths and licensed-victualler Smiths, Free Trade Smiths and Tariff Reform Smiths, must seek partners for life in their own particular section of the Smithian multitude. The Unionist Smith would not lead a Home Rule damsel to the altar, nor should Smith the tailor wed the daughter of a Smith who sold boots."

In its effect upon women the caste system has been most deleterious because of the difficulty of finding husbands within the same caste. It has led to the making away with undesirable daughters, which was frequently practised by the parents before the English Government stepped in and made female infanticide a crime and severely punished the culprits. Yet we are told that the disproportion of female to male children shows that the practice has not been completely stamped out, and that many fathers foreseeing the financial difficulties to be encountered in marrying their daughters, have deliberately made away with them at birth. In the smaller villages the crime is difficult of detection, but when the ratio of girls to boys falls particularly low in a community, the Government quarters extra police upon the people, making all the inhabitants contribute towards the cost of their maintenance, and the records soon show that girl babies are again being born in the villages.

Life in a high-caste Brahman family is much more complicated than that of the low-caste family, and many burdens are added to the already heavy ones borne by the Hindu woman, because of the rituals and customs woven around this caste system. A woman told me that she had a friend who lived in the house of two maiden aunts who were most orthodox Hindus. This woman was not allowed to touch a thing in the morning before her bath. Beside her bed was a long pole with which she must handle her towels and clothing, and she was not permitted to enter the presence of her aunts until her uncleanliness had been removed by ablutions and prayers.

The mother-in-law of my friend has practically no social intercourse with her son's wife because she has broken caste, eats with Europeans, and wears shoes made from leather. Her own mother at first felt her daughter's disgrace keenly, and would not see her for many years. At last love triumphed over custom, and now the mother will visit the daughter if assured that a place will be made ceremonially clean where she may spread her mat of holy dharba grass, on which she sits while chatting. She will receive nothing from the hand of her daughter, neither water nor food, and when she returns home she takes a complete bath and changes her wearing apparel that has become polluted by contact with her daughter's house.

Orthodox Hindus do not like sitting upon a mat of cloth or walking upon a carpet. In many houses a wooden bench or board is kept for visitors. The wife of a Resident in one of the Indian cities gave a reception to which came several ladies from the conservative Hindu families. They carefully avoided walking upon the rugs, and sat upon the edge of the chairs, looking most unhappy. The wife of the Resident asked an advanced Hindu lady why her afternoon was not a success so far as the Indian guests were concerned. She was told that the only thought that possessed these little women was a desire to get home. They wished to be polite and stay as long as etiquette demanded, but they welcomed with avidity the finality of the party when they might return and bathe and purify themselves from the close contact of foreigners and Mohammedans.

The members of the Brahmo Samaj, that progressive offshoot of Hinduism, have broken caste and allow their women to go about freely. I was in a town of Southern India with a member of this sect, and we called upon the head mistress of a large school for girls. She was at home with her newly born baby, waiting for the forty days of uncleanness to pass before returning to her school. She was a very intelligent woman, talking freely of the good and the bad of their social system. She said that a school for girls such as that of which she was the head, where four hundred young girls were being educated in modern thought, would have the greatest influence upon the women of the next generation, but that it would take time to eradicate the instincts of generations of ignorance and superstition, so deeply woven into the very nature of the Indian woman.

At the close of the visit the baby was brought to me, and rather lacking a subject for conversation I made the unfortunate remark to the baby, " You will grow up a good Hindu and stick to your caste." I was not prepared for the storm of protest it raised from my friend who had brought me to the home. She turned on me furiously and said : " How can you say such things, you, a modern woman? Caste is the ruin of India. If we want progress we must break caste : it is our only hope."

It is not caste alone that makes the rules that govern the life and actions of the Indian woman, but from birth to the burning-ground every detail of life is cast into a mould of ceremony and ritual, which in the hands of a less spiritual people would have degenerated into mere sham. Of the sixteen events in the life of a man, all are viewed from a religious aspect, and accompanied by a religious ceremony. The most sacred prayers are said in the morning before partaking of food, and it is the husband, the head of the house, who is supposed to say the prayers for all

beneath his roof-tree. " No sacrifice is allowed
to women apart from their husbands, no religious
rite, no fasting ; as far as a wife honours her
lord, so far is she exalted in heaven," says the
laws of Manu, yet the instinct of religion is
strong in the Hindu woman, as it is in women all
over the world, and they do perform a worship.
At the time of her marriage, at the marriage of
her children, and at many of the sacred feasts,
the wife must sit with her husband during the
time he is engaged in the performance of the
acts of worship, though she takes no active part
in the ceremonies. If a man has lost his wife,
he cannot perform the sacrifice of fire.

The Hindu woman has her gods, which she
keeps in the kitchen, the most sacred room in a
Hindu household. In all the time I was in
India I never saw the inside of the kitchen of
any of my Indian friends. I have been told
that it is divided into two parts, the smaller
room used for the cooking and as pantry for the
storing of food, and must be kept free from
ceremonial defilement. The larger half of the
kitchen of a middle-class household serves as
dining-room, and in an alcove or in one corner
are the household gods and the utensils to be
used in their worship. None of the images used
by a woman are consecrated, but she lights her
lamp and bows her head and prays for the safety
of her dear ones, then offers a bit of fruit or betel
or a sweetmeat that she has prepared, and
scatters sandal paste and coloured rice or the

petals of sweet-smelling flowers over her god. There is generally in each tiny yard or in the kitchen a tulasi plant, around which the women walk while chanting a prayer. This plant is considered the wife of Vishnu, and is revered by all. There are many blessings promised to one who attends and waters one of these plants, and it will keep care and tribulation from its worshippers and grant pardon to the sinner who cherishes the tulasi plant. Yet it is more particularly worshipped by women. At one time, it is said, women were commanded to walk around it one hundred and eight times each day, which certainly was a blessing from a hygienic point of view, as it gave exercise to these shut-in women, who are restricted to the four walls of their homes.

At night when the lamps are lighted the wife makes obeisance to the flame, saying—

> The flame of this lamp is the supreme good.
> The flame of this lamp is the abode of the Supreme.
> By this flame sin is destroyed,
> Oh, Thou light of the evening, we praise thee.

At the time of the evening meal the men have an elaborate religious ceremony, but the women say simply, " Govinda, Govinda," a name for Vishnu, before partaking of their food.

The devout mother teaches her children the tales of the gods, and at worship time when the bell is sounded they are taught to place their

hands together in the attitude of prayer and bow
their little heads to the gods. It is the
father who is expected to teach them the
Vedic texts and the truths to be found in
the Puranas.

The daily worship is held in the homes, but
on feast days or for especial acts of devotion,
such as prayers for the blessings of a son, or
the giving of thanks for favours received, the
women go to the temples. These are crowded
on holy days or days of anniversary of the gods.
No one ever goes to the temple empty-handed,
and one sees the little brass jar of holy water,
the wreath of marigold or sweet-smelling flowers
which are supposed to give pleasure to the
aesthetic senses of the gods. Many women take
a coconut to the temple, which fruit seems to be
generally connected with temple worship. The
breaking of the coconut is said to represent the
slaying of the sacrificial animal, which is only
done now in the temples dedicated to Kali, that
goddess of terror who delights in the blood of
her victims.

While in Benares I visited a temple dedicated
to Shiva, in which were several enormous bulls,
the animal sacred to this god. They were of a
bluish grey in colour, and from long living in
the temple had become as clever as the priests
in looking for offerings from their worshippers.
But while the priests looked for silver or gold,
the bulls had an eagle eye with which to discern
from afar the woman who carried a basket of

grain. They stood at the back of the temple and eyed each worshipper as she entered. If the pious woman had only a brass water-pot in her hand they did not move ; but if they saw a basket, they immediately started for her, and graciously allowed her to pour the grain into their open mouths, the woman taking care that she did not pollute the bulls by touching their lips with her hand. A wreath of marigolds was then thrown over the neck of the bull, the holy water was poured on his shoulders, and he returned to his place. I saw an old lady lovingly stroke the back of one of these pampered beasts, ending with the tail, the end of which she used to stroke her face, and afterwards lovingly kissed this appendage of her idol. The expression on her face was one of deepest reverence, and for her the great blue bull represented the god for whom her hungry soul was longing. The educated Hindu would say that she was struggling to find a god as are we all, but that she was still a child in matters spiritual and required a material representative of her ideal. They say that the real Hindu, the man who has studied the Vedas and understands the spirit of his religion, needs no images nor ritual. In his prayer he plainly shows that to him God is a spirit. He says—

Oh, Lord, pardon my three sins. I have in contemplation clothed Thee in form, who art formless ; I have in praise described Thee, who art ineffable ; and in visiting shrines I have ignored Thy omnipresence.

A HOLY MAN, BENARES.

To face p. 96.

In many of the temples, besides the priests to minister to the gods, are dancing girls, whose duties are to dance at the shrines, sing hymns, and generally delight the gods. They are a recognized religious institution, and are honoured next to the priests. They are obtained when quite young by purchase or by gift. Often in times of famine a girl is sold to the temple, that her price may save the rest of the family from starvation. One is given that all may live. In other cases a girl is often a thankoffering given to the gods because of recovery from sickness or great tribulation. A rich man, instead of presenting his own daughter, would buy the daughter of some poor family and present her. These girls, who have no word to say in regard to the disposal of their persons, are public women, and the gains of their profession go towards the support of the temple. If there should be children born to these professional dancing girls, they are brought up in their mother's profession, very much as were the children born to the priestesses of Aphrodite in the temples of Alexandria.

All Indian girls must be married, consequently these temple women are formally married to a dagger, a tree, or some inanimate object, who, as a husband, cannot object to the actions of his wife. Lately, in some places it has been made a criminal offence to sell a girl or give a daughter to a temple, and it is only done surreptitiously. One is told in India that it is a thing of the past, yet in one large temple in the South there are said to be over one hundred dancing girls kept for the amusement of the blasé gods.

These dancing girls share with their sisters, the nautch girls, the only real freedom given to Indian women. The latter are taught to read and write, to play musical instruments, and to make themselves attractive and charming to men. They come and go freely, mingling with both men and women. They are found at all feasts and public ceremonies, and have a very definite and honourable place in Indian society. Whatever discredit may be attached to her calling, she is considered a necessary adjunct to the temple and the home. Her presence at weddings is considered most fortunate, and in some castes it is the nautch girl who fastens the tali around the neck of the bride, a ceremony similar to placing the wedding-ring upon the finger. She holds the centre of the stage at all entertainments given in honour of guests. While we were in a native province ruled by a prince who had the reputation of liking wine, women, and song even more than did the average ruling prince in India, we were edified by the dancing of a woman brought from Bombay at the expense to the prince of nearly one hundred pounds a day.

The dancing is extremely modest, as the dancer is fully clothed, and it is the graceful, languorous poses of her slim body, the waving of her arms heavily laden with bracelets, and the slow moving, gliding steps that keep time to the tinkle

of the anklets, that charm her admirers. There
is a proverb that says, " Without the jingling
of the nautch girl's anklets, a dwelling-place does
not become pure."

CHAPTER VI

INDIAN HOME LIFE

ALTHOUGH the women are supposed to have no religious standing and are considered unfit to read the Vedas or touch the consecrated gods, still their entire life is influenced by religion or superstition, and the religion and superstition of the Eastern woman, of whatever land, is so inextricably entwined, that it is hard to tell where one leaves off and the other begins. Like her sisters of China and Egypt, she is afraid of the evil eye. She firmly believes that if her jewels, her dress, or her children are looked upon with jealous or covetous eyes, much sorrow will come to her, and she has many charms and ceremonies with which to counteract the baneful influence of spiteful persons. It is never wise for a visitor to regard a baby too closely or to admire its jewels or clothing openly, as, even if the mother is one of the advanced minority, instinct will assert itself, and deep within her heart, bred there by centuries of tradition, will be a little feeling that something *might* happen to her dear one. Quite likely, when the unwise caller departs, the mother

will make a lamp of kneaded rice flour and fill
it with oil or clarified butter, which, when lighted
and passed round the baby's head, will remove
the dreaded evil.

The Hindu woman's life is ruled by omens to
a far greater extent than is the life of the woman
of the Western world. If she is starting on a
visit to a friend, it is a very bad sign for her
to meet a widow, any one carrying a new pot, a
bundle of firewood, a pariah, a lame man, two
men quarrelling, a leper—in fact, there are about
a dozen things she should avoid, or else be under
the necessity of returning to her home and saying
a few prayers before daring to start on her
journey again. If she should sneeze once, it is
most unfortunate, and should be followed by a
second in order to avert the evil, but if the second
sneeze is followed by others, the more the better,
it is a most certain sign that her most ardent
wishes will soon be granted. When one yawns
it is polite to snap the fingers and say, " Govinda,
Govinda," as many believe that the life may
leave the body while yawning, and to avert this
calamity from a baby the mother snaps her
fingers and murmurs, " Krishna, Krishna," in its
tiny ears.

Mohammedan and Hindu customs are so much
alike that it is often hard to say that one is a
Mohammedan custom or that another is purely
Hindu. At the marriages, and the return of the
daughter to her home to give birth to her first
child, at the birth of the children, and in many

of the social customs of the Mohammedans are
seen the influence of the Hindu religion.   It was
the Mohammedans who brought the " purdah "
system, or the seclusion of women, into India.
Before the invasion of these warlike people the
women of India went about freely, but now
the Hindus are practically as secluded as are the
Mohammedan women.   In the North, where the
influence of the followers of the Arabian prophet
made itself most dominant, the women are much
more secluded than in the South, where the
Mohammedans did not come in such large
numbers.

It is in the villages that true India is to be
found, unchanging, languorous India.   Here is
a self-centered commonwealth, with little depend-
ence for its welfare upon the outer world, and the
people have remained the same as their fathers
and their father's fathers, impervious to new
innovations and ideas.   To look at one of these
villages is very different from ideas one may
have formed of them by reading books of travel.
The first impression received upon entering one
is that of an enlarged barnyard, as cows and
farm implements take entire possession of the
narrow streets.   The low, thatched mud houses
are without doors, windows, or chimneys.   The
floor is generally plastered with cowdung, which,
when dry, leaves a hard shellac-like polish, considered by the natives most sanitary.   It has to
be redone every two weeks, and to Western eyes
is a most unsightly operation, as it is done with

the hands of the housewife. It is said that when the Salvation Army sent its first volunteers to India, they required them to live the life of the Indian, and that this smearing of the earthen floors with the national substitute for varnish was one of the chief causes why women were not always ready to volunteer for service in the East.

There is virtually no furniture in the homes. The stove consists of three or four bricks, around which the fuel, consisting of dried cakes of mud and cowdung, are broken, and which smoulder rather than burn. A few earthenware pots and a large dish in which to serve the food, some brass utensils, and a large jar for carrying water, complete the culinary arrangements. For plates, banana or plantain leaves are used, or, lacking these, small leaves are sewn together. This saves the drudgery of washing dishes, as the leaves are thrown away after each meal, and the fingers are used in place of the knives and forks of the more aesthetic races. Chairs and tables are not needed, as the Indian squats upon his haunches, as only an Oriental can ; and in silence, regarding only his own food, to which he helps himself from the central dish, he eats his meal. When the lord of the household has finished, he graciously allows his wife to eat from the same leaf. No Indian woman who conforms to the customs of her race ever eats at the table with the men of her household, yet this is not confined to the women of India. The separation of the

men from the women at the dinner-table is practised by all Orientals. The women of China and
Japan eat with the younger children when the
master of the house has finished, and no Egyptian
husband, unless one of the small class who have
become thoroughly Westernized, would think of
inviting his wife to share with him his evening
meal.

In the village homes the man shows his
superiority also in the fact that the only bed in
the house of the peasant or workman is that for
the master, if bed it can be called—simply a rough
framework of wood with coir ropes strung across
it. The extra wardrobe of the family, if they
are so fortunate as to possess more than the one
garment which they wear, is hung on a pole in
a corner of the room, and need not take much
space, as the clothing of India's poor is scant—
a loincloth, a sheet for the shoulders, and a
long piece of cotton for the head suffices him.
His wife will only possess a tight-fitting little
bodice, and six yards of cloth which she will
drape gracefully around her body, making it
serve both as dress and head covering. Yet the
woman's arms are covered often with bracelets,
anklets tinkle as she walks, and as she draws her
sari across her face when passing the stranger,
the glint of a nose-ring is seen, or the light flashes
from a necklace that rests against her brown
skin. This jewellery may be of gold, silver,
brass, or even of glass, but the woman of the
village loves these aids to feminine charms as

well as does her city sister. In the olden time the peasant had no trust in banks, and when he accumulated a few extra rupees, he added a bangle to his wife's arm, or bought a nose or ear-ring. It served the double purpose of saving money which might be foolishly spent at the autumn fair, and also was easy to take to the moneylender in times of stress. There are many thousands of pounds of gold that go into India each year and disappear. The officials say it is turned into jewellery for these wives and daughters of India's great middle class, who seem never too poor to have a touch of gold or silver upon the persons of their womenfolk.

The village wife is relieved of the necessity of providing clothing for the children, because until they are seven or eight years old an amulet string or a silver anklet completes their ward-robe. There are many of these little brown bodies around every doorway, looking like dark-skinned cupids. One rarely sees a child in India with a bad skin, which perhaps is due to the oil-baths which they receive in early child-hood. Mothers bathe their babies in oil, then wash it off with a vegetable soap, leaving the skin soft and shining as satin. This is a luxury indulged in by older people also, and the giving of oils for the bath is a favourite present among friends.

In the shade of the porch is often seen a cradle, a very simple affair made of four pieces of wood with a hammock of cloth held between them.

Around the top of the cloth is arranged baby's toys so that he may lie and amuse himself, which is quite necessary where the mother has as many household duties to attend to as the Indian farmer's wife.   In places where the woman is working in the field, the baby may be seen wrapped in a hammock-like affair and tied to the limb of a tree ; and it is a common practice among labouring women, I am told, to give the babies a drug to keep them quiet while the mothers work.   Opium is very generally used in India, especially among the higher classes, although forbidden by both Hindu and the Mohammedan religion.   It is supposed to invigorate the aged, and an Indian told me that he thoroughly believed that all men after they pass the age of fifty were better for the moderate use of opium.

The wife of the village man or peasant is not " purdah nashim," or secluded, as is the wife of the rich man.   She takes her share in the agricultural work, besides carrying water from the village well, making the cakes of fuel and plastering them against the side of the house to dry, grinding the meal, husking the rice, washing the clothing, and cooking the meals.   Yet with all her work the monotony of her life is broken by many feasts and ceremonies in which she takes a part.   Each district and temple has its own particular fête day, and there are many family feasts where work is given up at the time of special rejoicing.   Relatives and friends meet together, the houses are decorated, bright saris are brought forth, and the time is spent in pleasure and merry-making. There are eighteen obligatory feasts in the year for the orthodox Hindu, but only a few of the principal ones are celebrated.

Many of the ceremonies in the home originated in sanitary laws, which would not have been obeyed unless the people were made to believe that they were of divine origin. At a certain time of the year when smallpox is rife, and the epidemic has passed, there is a worship of the " Mother," which requires the house to be thoroughly cleaned and purified, all the old vessels broken, all old clothing burned or placed in the sun for a certain time, before the women are permitted to go to the temple to worship their favourite goddess. There is another spring feast, when the women go down to the water dressed in yellow, and send small lighted lamps down the stream to the spring goddess. At the feast of the serpents the villagers take offerings to the sand-hills, and pour milk and honey into the holes where the snakes are supposed to dwell, asking protection of these gods of wisdom, who especially guard the eyes of their worshippers. At another feast the women take red water and sprinkle it upon each other, rejoicing over the slaying of the giant god of evil. The girls take part in a pretty feast in the fall, when they decorate their little brothers with flowers and garland the houses, and at night light innumer-

able little lamps, making a village look like a
miniature fairyland.

The village women appear rather sullen, but
when known they are found to be as happy as is
the wife of the average working man.   If there
is no drought drying up the crops, if no disease
comes to the cattle, if the moneylender is not
too avaricious, if a few pennies can be saved
to buy bracelets from the bangle-man at the
annual festival, and if the gods do not disgrace
her by sending too many daughters, she is happy.
Yet the village woman and her family are always
but half a step in advance of the waiting wolf ;
famine comes with swiftness, and quick deaths
from plagues to hundreds of thousands of these
peasant people, who constitute nine-tenths of the
population of India.

The life of the women in the small towns and
villages is like life in another world compared to
that led by the women in the large cities of
Calcutta or Bombay or Madras.   Here the Indian
lady seems to be trying to lose her national
characteristics, and Indian society is very disap-
pointing to a visitor from the West who wishes
to see something of the life lived by the lady of
India.   It seems to be merely a copy of the life
of the English society woman, and her day is
filled with teas, society concerts, and receptions.
Their homes are thoroughly English in every
department, their drawing-rooms are filled with
English bric-à-brac, they go to the entertainments in most luxurious motors ; their children,

dressed in European clothes, are brought down
to see the guest by an English governess, and
English is the language of the home.   Many of
the Indian women are members of clubs, musical
societies, and are taking active part in the
charities for the benefit of their people.

The Indian woman wields a strong influence
over her husband, and has more of a place in
the life around her than we imagine, from the
stories we hear of unhappy days spent " Behind
Zenana Bars."   We are apt to consider the
secluded, shut-in Eastern woman as a cowed,
frightened creature, afraid to say her soul is her
own, while among the better class, at least, it is
quite the contrary.   It takes a brave man to go
absolutely against the wishes of his womenfolk,
as they have the advantage of numbers in their
favour.   In every great household there are
innumerable women relatives, satellites, and
servants revolving around the personality of the
mistress.   These Eastern women have been
schooled in the art of intrigue and understand
thoroughly the efficacy of passive resistance.   If
the wife wishes to accomplish a certain object,
and is able to enlist the women of the household
on her side, the man will be compelled sooner or
later to submit to her wishes.

The older, conservative women are very tyrannical, and try their best to combat the newer
ideas brought to the zenanas by their sons and
daughters.   Many of the younger generation
are trying to break from the patriarchal custom

of all the family living under one roof.   They
say it is very fine in theory, and has worked with
good results in the villages, but that it has many
bad points, the chief of which is that it allows
no expression of individuality.   The personality
must be sunk in the family.   When all the men
will work and become producers and con-
tributors to the family fund, it makes for harmony
in the home, but when some are drones and live
on the toil of others, it makes the burden too
heavy for the few and causes quarrels and
dissensions.

Women are helpless in India in the earning of
a living for themselves, and if widowhood comes
they must depend for support on some male relative of their own or of the family of their
deceased husband.   I know a boy of eighteen
who is the only support of his wife, his aunt, a
widow, his widowed mother, and his young sister.
He was compelled to leave school and take a
position in an office in order to take care of all
these women, as he was the responsible head
of the family.   It is hard for a boy who is
ambitious and anxious to obtain an education,
when there are many women in his household, as
they care more for the immediate necessities than
for a prospective successful future.   They feel
that his father and his father's father were able
to provide for the wants of the family, so why
should the boys of to-day spend years in studying books when they might be adding to the
family exchequer?

It is the women who are compelling the younger boys and girls to conform to the old usages and traditions in regard to marriage. Many a boy leaves school and would like a chance to find a place for himself in life before burdening himself with a wife. But this he is not allowed to do. His mother believes that all boys should be married early in life, consequently the boy is saddled with a family at about the age when the American boy is taking his first shy look at the girl across the aisle in the schoolroom. These modern young men would also like to have a voice in the selection of their wives, but that also is denied them. They must conform to the traditions of their caste and the customs of their family. I know a boy who was compelled to marry his niece, although his education had taught him that these intermarriages were not for the good of his race; still, he was helpless, and could not successfully oppose the combined wishes of the women of his family.

Side by side with these Indian women who guard jealously the customs and traditions of other days are the Westernized society women, who seem to share with their husbands in the spirit of imitation that has entered into the very soul of the Indian people who have come into contact with the English. The Indian gentleman feels that he must talk " sport," the schoolboy prides himself upon the knowledge of cricket and football and talks the jargon of Eton and Rugby. Because the meat-eating Englishmen from cold, dreary England must exercise in order to live, the Indian also devotes himself to a strenuous regime that is absolutely alien to his habits and the requirements of his climate. The Indian lady, with her exaggerated English accent, and her costume that is neither of the East nor of the West, is a paradox. She may well be zealous in borrowing what she needs from the English, but it seems hard for her to assimilate what she takes and make it a part of herself. The affectations which she uses to show her cosmopolitanism are palpably grafted upon her tree of knowledge, and we who wish to see the real India are only consoled in the thought that these unusual conditions which prevail in the large cities are only the graftings, and that the tree itself is not affected by them. The real woman of India is bound to grow in knowledge brought by education and experience, but deep down in her heart she will be essentially the same for years to come. She will not try to exchange her personality for another's, even in outward appearance.

The dawn of consciousness that has been preceded by long twilight is now awakening in the soul of the Eastern woman, and she will see by its light that she has a strength and individuality of her own and that she need not mortgage her birthright to borrow alien charms from the women of other lands.

CHAPTER VII

MARRIAGE—THE GOAL OF WOMAN

THERE are three great events in a Hindu woman's life : first, her marriage ; second, the birth of her son ; and third, if she should be so unfortunate, her widowhood.

These three events are of immense importance to all women, but as a woman of the Far East is supposed to be created for one purpose only, the rearing of sons to her husband's house, marriage and birth of children assume a larger place in her life than in the life of the Western woman, where these two events are often merely incidents. Also when a Hindu woman marries she expects to stay married, as she cannot divorce her husband, and he can only divorce her for infidelity. Even death will not open for her the doorway to remarriage, because if her husband should die before her, she must remain true to his memory for life.

The woman's inclinations are seldom consulted, in regard to the choice of a husband, because, quite likely, when she is not much more than a child, her parents begin to look around for a

8

suitable alliance for her. Their choice must fall upon a man of the same caste, a relative if possible. The prospective bridegroom may be a young boy, or he may be an old man, a widower. The girl *must* be married. There are no reasons in the Hindu philosophy which allow a girl to pass the marriageable age without a husband being chosen for her. Men may become " sanyassis," that is, renounce the world and remain bachelors, but this is not allowed women under any circumstances, as they must fulfil their destiny, which is to be the mothers of men.

If a girl passes the marriageable age, if she should be twelve or thirteen without being settled in life, her family would feel that they were disgraced, and she would have slight opportunity for marriage in any respectable family. Therefore, it is incumbent upon her parents to find for her a husband as soon as possible, which leads to one of the greatest crimes against Indian womanhood—child marriages.

There are many preliminaries to be arranged before the final choice of a bridegroom is decided, but when he is found at last, the important question of the dowry arises. In some places the father of the bride gives a dowry with his daughter, in others the groom's father pays a certain sum to the parents of the little bride, practically buying her. Nearly every caste has a different mode of procedure regarding the exchange of presents and money.

The girl's personal jewellery and everything she receives from her future father-in-law, or that she takes with her to her new home, are most clearly set down, article by article, in a document, and constitute her own personal property, which she may claim if she becomes a widow.

Marriage is a most ruinous operation financially for the parents, especially for the father of the bride. He must give a feast lasting for five days to all friends and relatives, presents to all the contracting parties, and great liberality must be shown the Brahmins and priests who assist in the ceremony. If his new son-in-law is an educated youth, he will demand a much larger dowry with his bride, in these days when Western education is meaning so much in the life of the Indian youth. If he is a " failed B.A.," he may only demand, we will say, one thousand rupees from his father-in-law. If he successfully passed his examinations and is a full B.A., he quite likely would feel that those letters added to his name were worth at least two thousand rupees ; and if he should by chance be a Doctor of Laws, his demands might be limited only by the knowledge of the amount of gold the father of his bride has stored for this emergency.

After the preliminary ceremonies have been concluded and the family priest has decided upon the most propitious day for the nuptials, the family begin to make preparations for the wedding. Invitations are taken to friends and relatives who are within visiting distance by the women of the household, who make upon the forehead of the invited female guest the round red caste mark, and leave a small bundle of pan leaves and betel-nut for the other members of the family. Often a little sandalwood paste is touched to the chin and between the shoulders by the bearer of the invitation. Mohammedan ladies send a tiny mica box with a cardamom seed in it and a piece of confectionery, which is given with the verbal invitation by the messenger, who must, if possible, be some member of the family instead of a servant.

In the case of rich people the strong box is opened and the hoarded rupees brought forth with which to buy the gold and silver jewellery for both bride and groom, the elaborate wedding garments, and the saris, which are given as presents to the women guests, and shawls for the men ; the store-rooms are examined to make sure that there is rice in plenty, also wheat flour, butter, oil of sessaman, peas, vegetables, fruits, pickles, curries, in fact, all the many foodstuffs necessary in the preparation of the elaborate feasts which are the main events of the wedding. Sandalwood powder is bought in great quantities, antimony for the eyes, incense, the red paste which wives use on the forehead, and innumerable numbers of the beautiful flower wreaths with which the guests are garlanded after the entertainments. Plenty of new earthen dishes are selected from the potters' store, for these vessels may never be used the second time.

In the case of the poor man, now is the time when the visits are made to the moneylender, because, rich or poor, prince or peasant, there must be no question of stint at this time of rejoicing.

A wedding is a very gorgeous affair, being limited only by the means of the contracting parties, but it is generally conceded that all Indians, of whatever class of society they may be members, spend far too much upon the nuptials of their children.

Each one of the five days has its especial religious rite. One ceremony typifies the giving of the girl by the father to the husband and the renunciation of his parental authority. On another day the husband fastens the tali around his young wife's neck, which is practically the same as placing the marriage-ring upon the finger of the new bride. This tali is a small gold ornament strung on a little cord composed of one hundred and eight very fine threads closely twisted together and dyed yellow with saffron. Before tying the tali it is taken to the guests, both men and women, who bless it. Old ladies whose husbands are alive are specially requested to bless the tali, in order to insure the couple a long married life. This symbol of wifehood is tied with three knots, thus trebly ensuring the marriage tie, and is never to be removed unless the wearer is so unfortunate as to become a widow, when the cord is cut. The most unkind thing one woman can say to another is, " May your tali be cut ! "

After the tying of this emblem the newly married couple walk three times around a lighted fire, which is the ultimate binding of the marriage contract, for there is no more solemn engagement than that which is entered into in the presence of fire. Rice is thrown over the pair, and they throw it upon each other, signalling that they hope to enjoy an abundance of this world's goods and a fruitful union. Rice is used at weddings in nearly all Eastern countries as typifying prosperity and fruitfulness, and it is perhaps from the Far East that we borrow our custom of throwing rice upon the newly married pair.

Many Hindu women wear, in addition to the tali, an iron bracelet to indicate their marriage state. Among the rich it is gilded and, consequently, not easily distinguished from the many bracelets that always cover the Indian lady's arm.

A young Hindu boy is not supposed to chew betel-nut nor put flowers in his hair until he is married. On the fourth day of the marriage festivities the groom is given his first betel-nut by his brother-in-law, and his head is wreathed with flowers. In a few castes the bride has her left nostril bored on the fifth day of the marriage and an ornament placed therein. After marriage in some parts of India the woman wears a streak qf red powder in the parting of her hair, and in practically all provinces she wears the little round mark of wifehood between the eyes, which, as age comes, is elongated, until gradually, by the time that children and grandchildren cluster around her knee, the little red mark has grown into a straight line, losing itself in the whitening locks. In Mysore and in some of the southern provinces a woman does not tuck up her dress in the back until she is married.   Then an end of the long sari, which is twisted several times around the body, is brought from the front to the back and tucked into a belt, forming a sort of trousers, and incidentally exposing more brown leg than we women of the Western world think consistent with modesty.

At the final feast the bride and groom eat together from the same leaf to show their complete union.   This is the first and last time that the wife will eat in company with her husband, if he is an orthodox Hindu and not imbued with the new Western ideas.   Always, in the future, she will serve him his meal, and after he has finished she will eat with the other women of the household and the smaller children, using the same leaf which has done service for her lord and master.

When all the religious rites are finished and the festivities have come to an end, there is a final procession, when the wife and husband, gorgeously arrayed in all their jewellery, are carried round the town to the accompaniment of music, the explosion of fire crackers, the shooting of rockets, and the shouting of friends. Then, if the bride is still a child, she returns home with her parents, who keep her secluded until the time arrives for her to return to her husband's home and fulfil the duties of a wife. The day the husband and mother-in-law come to take the wife to their home is made another time of rejoicing. She remains with them for a month when she revisits her old home, and often for the first few years, or until she has children, she lives alternately in her husband's house and in that of her parents. If she finds herself ill-treated by her husband and tormented by her mother-in-law, the young girl often seeks her father's home for shelter and protection, and remains with them until the husband or his mother come in person to persuade her to return home. Nearly always her family add their persuasions, if not their force, to compel the wife to return to her husband's roof, as it is a great disgrace to all concerned to have a wife leave her husband. After the children come, the wife rarely leaves her house and devotes her time and energies to the rearing of the little ones that fill all homes, from the mansions of the rich to the huts of the poor peasants. There seem to be more little brown bodies in India than in any place I have visited, unless I except China, where the staple articles are rice and babies.

The new wife has to accommodate herself to
the customs of her husband's family, and much
of her future happiness depends upon the women
members of the household. If it is a very aristocratic family, she may have all the luxuries of
life, beautiful gold-embroidered saris, jewels,
servants, and slaves, but very little liberty. There
is a saying that you can tell the degree of a
family's aristocracy by the height of the windows
in the home. The higher the rank, the smaller
and higher are the windows and the more
secluded the women. An ordinary lady may
walk in the garden and hear the birds sing and
see the flowers. A higher grade lady may only
look at them from her windows, and if she is a
very great lady indeed, this even is forbidden
her, as the windows are high up near the ceiling,
merely slits in the wall for the lighting and
ventilation of the room.

There are many rules of etiquette prescribed
for the young girl-wife if she would show that
she has been properly trained by her parents.
For example, she must never speak of her
husband by name, nor may she use a word with
the same syllable as her husband's first name.
A friend of mine has a husband whose name
begins with the same syllable as that used in the
word sugar. She always speaks of sugar as " the
substance you put in your tea," and she generally
refers to her husband as " he." Nor would the
man say " my wife," but " my house," or some
word denoting the home. A man in Hyderabad

met his doctor on the street and said, " I wish you would come and see me. My house has a boil on its neck."

This same wife would not sit in the presence of her mother-in-law or her husband if others were present. It would show extreme lack of respect ; nor would she speak if her husband were in the room. We called upon the wife of a high official of Bangalore, who came into the room with her daughter-in-law and her young daughter, an extremely pretty girl. The daughter-in-law would not sit down in the presence of her husband's mother, nor did she speak, and looked extremely awkward and self-conscious, as she stood with her sari drawn across her mouth and watched us with her big black eyes. The little daughter played the veena, the national instrument, and as she sat upon the rug, gorgeously arrayed in an elaborate red and gold sari, with jewellery on arms, neck, ankles, toes, and with diamonds in each tiny nostril, she made a picture never to be forgotten.

In some of the big households where the sons bring their wives to live beneath the family roof-tree, the married quarters are not large enough to allow a separate room for each couple, and the women sleep in one room and the men in another. The mother has the right of assigning the couples who are to inhabit the married quarters for the week. But even the eagle eye of the mother-in-law cannot always watch the young people, and many a girl-wife steals across the courtyard to find her husband, who is waiting for her in the shadows. A crowd of young men in a school were asked to give their idea of what was the most beautiful music in the world. One answered, " The song of the bul-bul," another, " The plaintive strains of the zither," a third, " The cry of the night bird," but a young bridegroom said, " The music of my wife's anklets as she tries to suppress their sound when she steals to meet me in the moonlight."

One is amazed at the amount of jewellery worn by the Indian women, yet this vanity is not confined solely to the women, as in some of the provinces nearly every man has a jewel in his ear, and many of them wear most expensive finger-rings. The women excel in the artistic use of jewellery that on other people would seem tawdry and barbaric, but on these dainty little women is most becoming to their rich, dark beauty. Jewellery is not only worn by the lady, but women of every class are covered with it. The village woman will have perhaps but one cotton sari, and her home would be merely a mud hovel, but she will clink as she walks, and you know she wears silver anklets, and as she moves her sari to peep at you, you see the glisten of a bracelet. It may be of brass or it may be of silver, or, if she be very poor, coloured glass bangles will satisfy her cravings for the beautiful, and her arms will be covered with these ornaments from the wrist to the elbow.

At a railway-station near Baroda I saw women

whose legs to the knee were covered with huge brass bands that must have been, most inconvenient and heavy to carry. In Poona we stopped to watch a merchant of toe-rings place his wares upon his patron's toes which were held out to him for the purpose. The rings were so tight that soap had to be used to force them over the twinging toes. The operation was most painful to vanity, judging from the faces of the victims, but evidently the sight of the shining ring as they trudged down the dusty road repaid them for the suffering they had undergone. In this same market were innumerable booths for the sale of the glass bracelets that are worn by all the women of India, with the exception of widows. I watched an old woman in the bangle bazaar working them over the hands of the women who sat on the ground in front of her, prepared to spend unlimited time in acquiring these articles of adornment. The purchaser made her choice from the green or gold or red bangles piled carelessly upon the trays in front of her, then the bangle-seller squeezed and manipulated the hand, slowly working, pushing, coaxing the bangle over the hand, until finally it was on the arm, where evidently it would remain.

My husband and I dined with a Mohammedan who, after dinner, asked me into the zenana to meet his wife. The bareness of my arms shocked her, and she insisted upon presenting me with three bracelets for each arm, working them on so skilfully that it did not pain me, but on arriving at the hotel I found I could not remove them. I tried to persuade the Indian servant to break them for me, but he was horrified and said it would bring me very bad luck, as only widows had them broken on the arm. I feared I would be compelled to wear them all my life as my husband would not break them, having overheard the remarks about the widow. Finally I broke them myself, much to the detriment of my arms, which carried the scars for many days.

There is an immense amount of money going into India each year that never gets into circulation, as the gold coins are strung upon chains or melted to make the bracelets for the women and children. Life could be made much more comfortable for the Indian peasant if he would turn the money invested in jewellery for his womenfolk into comforts for the home.

The Hindu woman has few legal rights. Any property which her husband wishes to leave her must be given to her in his lifetime, as she cannot inherit his estate, but she may claim maintenance from his heirs, and if she should survive her son, she may become his legal heir. The male relatives are supposed to provide maintenance for the women of the family.

An outsider looking upon the Hindu home does not see where real union can possibly exist between a husband and wife. This is especially true at the present time, when nearly all the better class of India's sons are being educated, and are reading, listening, touching hands with the outside world. The women of the middle and lower classes, except in rare cases, are practically without education, few being able to read or write. The signs point to the fact that they will not long remain in this ignorant state, because the young men are demanding educated wives, and a desire for education is abroad in the land, although an old proverb says that to educate a woman is like placing a knife in the hands of a monkey. The English Government is establishing schools for girls in every town and village, and in Baroda enforced schooling is demanded for girls as well as for boys. But because of the early marriage of the girl, she has little opportunity of becoming a real companion to her husband, as he may continue his studies for years, while, when she becomes a wife, her schooldays are over.

I met a gentleman of about fifty years of age in the South of India who asked me to call upon his wife, a young girl of seventeen years, who became his bride at the age of twelve. She was not at all what the average girl of seventeen years would be in England or America. She was the polite hostess, with no trace of self-consciousness or gaucherie, graceful in her every movement. She was exquisitely dressed and covered with jewels. Large diamond clusters were in her ears, diamonds in each nostril, and around her neck a chain of rubies with a large pendant of pearls. Her manners were charming, and as we were parting she excused herself for a moment then returned to the room with a small tray on which was the red powder for the caste mark, betel-nut, fruit, and a small bouquet of flowers. She came to each of us and bowed, then with her right hand made the mark of wifehood upon our foreheads, and handed us the betel-nut and flowers. This gracious and pretty service is one of the many little kindly acts that are always performed by the hostess herself, as it would not be polite to delegate it to a servant.

I was charmed with this dainty little woman, yet I could not help thinking that she might be a pretty toy, but not a companion to the man with whom I had been conversing a few hours previous, and in whose library I had seen Emerson's "Essays," Farrar's "Life of Christ," "Pilgrim's Progress," the works of Tolstoy, Epictetus, and lying upon the desk, as if just left by the master, Maeterlinck's "Life and Death."

According to the ethical, moral, and religious standards of the Hindus, man and woman are equal. The Vedas teach—

Before the creation of this phenomenal world, the first born Lord of all creatures divided his own self in two halves so that one half should be male and the other half female. Just as the halves of fruit possess the same nature, the same attributes and the same properties in equal proportion, so man and woman, being the equal halves of the same substance, possess equal rights, equal privileges, and equal power.

This sounds very well in print, and learned Hindus quote us the Vedas to show that in their country women and men are considered equal. They are most indignant at the conception by the Western people of the treatment accorded the Indian woman by her husband. They say that books are filled with the stories of the brutality of husbands who marry these girl-wives without love on either side, yet they point out that it is a well-known fact that there are fewer wife-beaters in India than there are in England. Manu, the great law-giver, says, " A woman's body must not be struck hard even with a flower, because it is sacred."

In the olden time we are told that women were well versed in the Vedas, although it is now claimed that they are forbidden to read them or to be taught their truths. It is known that two of the famous songs of the Rig Veda were revealed by women, and when Sankaracharya, the great commentator of the Vedanta, was discussing this philosophy with another savant, a Hindu lady well versed in the Hindu scriptures was requested to act as umpire.

Whatever may have been her position in former times, at present there is no woman on earth who reveals more true attachment and devotion to her husband than does the Hindu wife. There is a beautiful saying, " Man is strength, woman is beauty ; he is the reason that governs and she is the wisdom that moderates."

In the Mahrabarata we find this definition of
a woman—

> A man's wife is his truest friend;
> A loving wife is a perpetual spring
> Of virtue, pleasure, wealth; a faithful
> Wife is his best aid in seeking Heavenly bliss.
> A sweetly speaking wife is a companion
>   In solitude, a father in advice,
> A mother in all seasons of distress,
> A rest in passing through life's wilderness.

CHAPTER VIII

INDIAN MOTHERHOOD

WHEN it is known that the girl-wife is to fulfil her destiny by giving her lord a child, she becomes a person of importance in her home circle, and there are endless ceremonies to be observed. Feasts are given friends, and many days are passed in rejoicing. One of the earliest celebrations is given the children of all friends and relatives, when the glass-bangle man comes with his wares, which are bought and freely distributed to the guests. About two months before the baby is expected the mother takes the daughter to her home, where she remains until after the formal purification, which is forty days after the birth of a girl, and thirty should she be so fortunate as to give a man-child to the world. At the end of that time her husband or his mother must come and take her home again. It would be an insult to send a lesser person, unless it were absolutely impossible for either of them to be the messenger. This custom of the young mother giving birth to her first child under her own family· roof-tree is followed by. Mohammedans as well as by Hindus.

The midwife in the villages is generally the wife of the barber, and naturally her knowledge of medicine is very much limited. She is ruled entirely by superstition and old-time custom. Her chief knowledge consists in different prayers, and a woman who is an expert in this field of obstetrics is always in demand, because there is no time when prayers are a greater necessity than at the birth of a child. Both the baby and its mother are peculiarly susceptible to the evil eye, to the influences of lucky and unlucky days, and a thousand other superstitions that make this time of a woman's life one of great danger. Happily for Indian women, the Marchioness of Dufferin, and the wives of other viceroys, have taken the cause of Indian womanhood to heart, and have established hospitals for women and supply nurses for the home. There are nearly two hundred and fifty hospitals and dispensaries throughout India, and women doctors with degrees from the highest institutions in Europe are giving their life to help the women of India. These doctors, with their assistants, their native students, and trained nurses, during the year 1903 took care of a million and a half of girls and women. Yet there is a vast opportunity for the enlarging of the work, as I was told that there are still a hundred million people who have no knowledge of the blessings to be obtained from European medicine and surgery, but who depend entirely upon the native doctors and midwives.

Many hospitals are maintained by missionaries, who have always been the forerunners in work to help the helpless, and it will only be a question of time when the mothers of India will not be compelled to be sacrificed to the superstition and ignorance of the women who are the only ones allowed near them in their time of travail. Even the most advanced men in India to-day would hardly allow a man doctor to attend his wife at the birth of a child. He would rather lose the life of the wife than so violate the customs of his class.

When the child is born, the date of the month, the hour of the day, and the star that is in the ascendant are carefully noted in order that the guru, or family priest, may cast the horoscope. Many of these astrologers are astute humbugs, and impose upon the credulity of their patrons to an enormous degree.

The house where a child has been born, as well as those who live in it, are considered impure for ten days, unless it is a rented house, when only the room in which the mother lies is unclean, and into which no one can enter except the midwife. The room is kept extremely warm, and incense is burned in it every day, and leaves are hung in front of the door to ward off evil spirits. On the eleventh day the linen and clothing is sent to the washman, and the mother, taking the child in her arms and with the husband

CRADLE IN VILLAGE, BARODA.

To face p. 132.

sitting beside her, goes through the ceremony of purification by the family priest, after which he purifies the entire household and the rooms. Still the mother is not supposed to receive her friends, and must keep apart from the rest of the family until the thirty or forty days are passed, when she passes through another purification ceremony, and then goes to the temple to offer sacrifice. Even the little baby is considered impure for twenty days, and must not be touched unless clothed in silk or woollen.

The new-comer has a succession of ceremonies to celebrate his arrival into this world of sorrows. On the twelfth day he is named ; on a later day, the first bracelets are put upon his arms and tiny anklets upon his ankles. When he is six months old he is given his first food. Five kinds of syrup are made, and the baby is given a taste of each one, and rice is put into his mouth. The father offers sacrifice to the household gods, the first loin-cloth is tied on the little man, the women sing, music is played, and feasting is indulged in by all. Each event is made the occasion of an elaborate feast, to which friends and relatives are invited and presents are given to the guests and to the priests. In fact, the priests seem to be omnipresent at all occasions in a Hindu family. A woman whom I was visiting was complaining of the many ceremonies that had taken place in her family during the past year, and she said that she was thoroughly tired of the worry and expense connected with them.

I said : " But who benefits by these elaborate feasts and rituals that give so much trouble and cause such an outlay in presents and money? " She said wearily : " Who benefits? Why, the priests and the Brahmins. They always reap their harvest, whether we are born, marry, or die. If we are wicked, we must ask them to intercede for us ; if we are good, we must ask them to thank the gods for us ; and if we die, they must help us across the river of fire. We can do nothing of ourselves ; they are our task-masters with ever-open palm."

If the newborn son survives the first two years—and the mortality of babies is frightful, especially in the cities—he will quite likely have the opportunity of having the tonsure made for the first time, and this event is only rivalled by the entertainment given when, whether boy or girl, the ears are pierced by the goldsmith and it is announced that babyhood is passed. These endless feasts would be ruinous to the poor Hindu were it not for the fact that it is practically the only time when he entertains his friends. There is no promiscuous dinner-giving as among the Western people ; friends are invited only in connection with some religious rite or to inaugurate a special event in the family.

If a member of one of the higher castes, the mother who has watched her baby grow from babyhood into boyhood, looks forward to the most solemn and important event in his life, the

ceremony called " the introduction to knowledge,"
when he is invested with the sacred cord. This
ceremony lasts from four to five days and is
nearly as expensive as a wedding. The father
must provide many pieces of cotton cloth and
small gold and silver coins to be given as presents
to the guests. He must have unlimited food
and a great collection of pottery, because, as at a
marriage feast, the dishes are broken after their
first use.

This cord may be seen on all Brahmins and
on the members of a few of the higher castes,
hanging from the left shoulder to the right hip.
It is composed of three strands of cotton, each
strand formed by nine threads. The cotton with
which it is made must be gathered from the
plant by the hand of a Brahmin, and corded and
spun by persons of the same caste, in order that
it may not be defiled by passing through the
hands of persons who are ceremonially unclean.
For a young boy the cord has only three strands,
but after he is married it is composed of six
strands and may have nine. It is symbolical of
the body, speech, and mind, and when the knots
are tied, means that the man who wears the
thread has gained control over these three organs
that cause all worldly troubles.

At the end of the ceremony the guests accom-
pany the boy, who is elaborately dressed and
seated in an open palanquin, through the streets
to the sound of singing, music, and merry-
making. On his return to his home, he, for the

first time, performs the sacrifice of fire, showing that he is now a member of his caste and
a twice-born son of India.

If the mother belongs to a poor family, quite
likely her boy will work to earn a few annas
to add to the family exchequer, or if they are
farmers, his days will be passed in the fields
frightening the greedy crows from the ripening
crops or driving away the animals that infest
the fields which are near the jungles. In
Baroda, education is compulsory ; but many a
mother gets around the law by paying the fine
of two rupees a month, and selling her small
boy's labour for five rupees, thus gaining a
livelihood.

England has established free schools in every
town and village, and there is little excuse even
for the boy or girl of poor parents not to have an
education. Even members of the depressed
classes, or, as they are called, the pariahs, have
their schools. The question that is agitating
the minds of the educators is what form of education should be given these sons of a people who
have been practically slaves for many centuries.
Many contend that they should have only a
technical education, that the sons of the carpenter
caste should be made better carpenters, and that
they should not be made barristers. A lady said
to me : " Said, my sweeper's son, goes to school,
and after getting an education he naturally feels
himself better than his father, a sweeper, or his
uncle, who is my groom. He cannot affiliate

himself with a higher caste than that into which he was born, as they will not accept him, and he has outgrown his own caste. What is he to do? He puts on a foreign hat and leaves his home, and in the next census, drops his name of Said Faruki and becomes John James Jones, a half-caste, and the census-taker wonders why there has been such an increase in half-castes. The population of half-castes grows from the lower castes who wish to raise themselves, but it is kept down in the census returns by the half-castes who wish to better themselves socially, and call themselves Portuguese or subjects of some other dark-skinned race of Europeans."

This question of the education of the Indian youth is a very serious problem with which those who have the welfare of India at heart have to contend. Many a boy when he returns to his home and his people says: "Why did they educate me?" There are few avenues of livelihood open to the Indian boy, as there is no Army or Navy or Church in which to enlist so many of the younger sons as in England or America. The main prizes are the Government offices, and failing these, the chief desire of all Indians is to be a lawyer. There are few places in the Government employ now, and the country is flooded with impecunious barristers.

The Indian feels that he has a real grievance in the question of the Civil Service examinations. For the higher positions in this service it is necessary for the student to go to England and obtain his degree at an English university. The question of expense is a bar to the great majority. One often hears of parents mortgaging their homes and practically selling themselves to the moneylender for life, that the boy may have this one great opportunity. If he wins, they have not struggled in vain, but if he fails, life will be very grey and grim, because quite likely his life and his son's, and his son's son's life will be given in a vain attempt to get rid of the burden of debt which seems to always hang over the heads of India's poor.

The question of the education of the daughter is not so much a matter of thought to the middle-class Mohammedan or Hindu mother, because at the time when, if she were in Western lands, she would be taking her books under her arm and starting for her first day at school, in India she is getting married. She may, if in a village, attend the school with her brothers until she is eight or nine years old, but rarely, except in the highest classes, does the little girl have a longer opportunity for study. In the cities the rich families are sending their daughters to private schools, and the Oriental home is the happy hunting ground for the English governess, who is engaged to teach, not only the knowledge to be found in books but also the etiquette to be observed in English society, as it seems to be the main object in life of the educated Indian, both man and woman, to be more English in manner than are the English themselves.

In all the better class homes the piano is seen, and seldom now does the daughter of the house play upon the veena or any instrument of Indian music. In Calcutta I went to a reception given by a great Indian lady. With the exception of the costumes worn by the pretty dark-eyed Bengalis, and the absence of men, I would have thought I was in an English house at an afternoon tea. English was spoken by nearly every one, the music was European, the refreshments were from an English caterer, and there was no distinct note of India in all the afternoon's ceremonies. Most of the ladies wore high-heeled French slippers, and many of them had their beautifully draped saris twined around bodies held in place by the French corset, which must have been most uncomfortable for these people, used to untrammelled freedom in regard to their dress.

Times are changing so fast in India that it is hard to say " This is a custom " or " That is a custom." Education is opening the eyes of the younger generation of Indian women to the fallacy of many of the old-time rites and superstitions. Still, many of the mothers are conservative and feel keenly their daughter's departure from the beliefs of her day, yet the pressure is so strong that many of these conservative mothers are sending their daughters to the schools, both mission and Government, where in the former they avail themselves eagerly of the education, but are not influenced by the religious teaching.

One devout Mohammedan mother said to me: "Yes, I send my daughter to a mission school, as it is the best in our town. I feel that they cannot hurt her, as she has had a good religious training in the home."

A great many of the mothers feel that the present system of education for women in India is wrong, and that the text-books are not the ones that should be adopted for the use of Indian children. The stories have little to do with Indian life, and the children do not understand them. For instance, stories of snowstorms, ice, and things that are to be seen in a foreign land, are far above the understanding of the average Indian girl. It is also said that the girl is taught of Joan of Arc and of English heroines, but nothing is said of the heroines of Indian history, nor is anything taught of Indian history before the English occupation. There is nothing given the child to inspire a feeling of patriotism, nor is she given any moral training except in the mission schools. She is given a certain amount of book knowledge, which quite likely she cannot assimilate, and is considered educated. I remember visiting a girls' school where the teacher asked a class of girls to recite Wordsworth's poetry, extracts from Shelley and Keats; they could tell the place of birth and give the list of English poets and chronology of the English kings most glibly, but what actual good it afforded the Indian girl to have all these interesting facts in her little head I could not see.

The Indian girl learns easily and is often most eloquent. There are no better public speakers than are the Bengali women, who seem to share with their men in the alertness of their brain. A prominent educator of India said :—

I have come in contact with people from all over the world in my capacity as educator, but I believe there are no men of any country who can compare with the Indian in quickness of thought and in capacity to learn. Within the small round head of the Bengali is a dynamo of resistless energy, that is for ever working, either for good or bad, but which ever way it turns, we of England must recognize its power.

The crying need of India is the great teacher, both man and woman ; the teacher who will really take an interest in his pupils and not feel the bar of race. This is the fault of the average man who comes to India, and if he does not have it when he arrives he soon acquires a pride in being one of the ruling race. The Indian boy and girl are extremely clever, and feel instantly this racial prejudice of the Englishman, and consequently resent his attitude of superiority. Tennyson's indictment of English schoolmasters could be justly applied to many of the teachers in India to-day :—

Because you do profess to teach, and teach us nothing, feeding not the heart.

There are wanted teachers who will give the Indian boy and girl the true value of an education other than its advantages from an economic standpoint. That must be considered also, and in a land where the crowds are great and famines many, it assumes even a larger importance in the lives of the boys who must become the wage-earners, than it does in Western lands, where life is not such a fierce struggle for the necessities. But along with the training for the making of a livelihood should be given another training. These boys and girls of India who are just start-ing on the road that their Occidental brothers and sisters have been treading for many generations should be given the broader view of education, its worth and meaning. They should be taught by loving teachers the true knowledge of which so beautiful a definition is given by Bishop Mant :—

> What is true knowledge ! Is it with keen eye
>   Of Lucre's sons to thread the mazy way ?
>   Is it of civil rights, and royal sway,
> And wealth political, the depths to try?
> Is it to delve the earth, to soar the sky?
>   To marshal nations, tribes in just array ;
>   To mix and analyze, and mete and weigh
> Her elements, and all her powers descry?
> These things, who will may know them, if to *know*
>   Breed not vainglory ; but, o'er all, to scan
> God in his works and Word shown forth below,
>   Creation's wonders and Redemption's plan ;
> Whence came we, what to do, and whither go :
>   This is true knowledge, and the whole of man.

CHAPTER IX

WOMAN'S SORROW

ABBE DU BOIS says : " The happiest death for a woman is that which overtakes her while she is still in a wedded state. Such a death is looked upon as a reward of goodness extending back for many generations ; on the other hand, the greatest misfortune that can befall a wife is to survive her husband."

Death is a tragedy in all lands, but with the Hindus it is made doubly tragical because of superstition and the endless ritual connected with their religion. The idea of mourning is not so much sorrow as it is uncleanness, defilement.

When death seems imminent the family priest is summoned to administer the last sacrament. The dying person is lifted from the couch and laid upon the ground, which has been made ceremonially pure by, smearing it with cowdung and by placing the sacred dharba grass upon it. It is said that if a man dies upon a bed he must carry it through eternity. It is most important that a man should breathe his last upon the earth, and not within the house, as there are certain phases of the moon when it would be a serious annoyance for all within the house to have a death beneath the roof. In fact, it pollutes the whole neighbourhood to have a death in the vicinity, and the neighbours share in the unclean state of the family until the corpse is carried to the burning-ground. Often if a death occurs in a house in an unpropitious phase of the moon, the dwelling must be vacated until such time as the priest shall permit it to be purified ; sometimes the ban cast upon the place lasts from three to six months.

The duration of the state of ceremonial impurity varies according to the age of the deceased. In the case of mere infants the time is about one day. In the case of a boy who has not been invested with the sacred cord, or a girl not married, the time is three days ; and after that, in either case, the time is ten days. In the case of a married girl, whether or not she has gone to live with her husband, her own people must observe the ceremonial for three days. During these periods the near relatives of the dead are unclean and their touch would defile any person or thing. They must not enter their own kitchen nor touch any cooking utensil. The food must be cooked by some one not personally connected with the dead, but of equal caste. If for some reason the mourning family cannot get any one of their own caste to cook for them, they must procure kitchen utensils and cook their food in some place other than the

usual kitchen, not using the utensils again.   If
a person in mourning went into a kitchen or
storehouse, everything would have to be thrown
away immediately.

The wailing of the women tells the story of
a death, as they abandon themselves completely
to their sorrow, tearing their hair, striking their
foreheads, and uttering shrill cries to show their
desolation.   As soon as the breath leaves the
body preparations are made at once for its disposal, as a corpse is never kept longer than
twenty-four hours in this hot climate.   The eldest
son, if there is one of suitable age, or the father
or eldest brother in order of nearest relationship,
or the husband if the deceased is a woman, must
conduct the funeral ceremonies.   The body is
washed and shaven and adorned with the marks
of his caste, and placed in a sitting position,
with the head uncovered, and the son or heir
performs a sacrifice before it.   Then the two
thumbs and the great toes are tied together and
the body is enveloped in a new white cloth and
placed upon a bier, formed of two long poles
with seven cross-pieces.   With the heir at the
head, carrying a pot of fire, the procession starts
for the burning-ground.   This bier must always
be carried by relatives or members of the same
caste.   When a man is ill and it is necessary to
tell him that he will soon depart from this world,
it is broken to him gently by some one saying,
" You will soon ascend a palanquin carried by
bearers of your own caste."   On the way to the

cemetery the procession is stopped three times and the bier placed on the ground, the face un-covered, and a prayer is said. If, as sometimes occurs, the person is not really dead and he revives, it is most unfortunate for all concerned, the revived man included, as he is considered as dead and not allowed to return to his home or to his caste.

Arrival at the burning-ground, where the funeral pile has been prepared by men whose profession it is to attend to the dead, and who are always of the pariah class, the untouchables, the body is put on the pyre and the sacred thread and loin cloth are removed with the winding-sheet, as the body must depart from the world in the state in which it entered it, completely naked. The head should be placed towards the south and the legs towards the north. If near a sacred river, like the Ganges, the body is laid for a few moments with the feet in the sacred water, and water is sprinkled over it. The heir performs the sacrifices, and it is he who sets the pile alight, while the priests repeat the prayers for the dead. After the pyre is lighted the family retire to a distance and leave the body to the administrations of the men in charge. In some places the heir is supposed to break the skull so that the gases may escape and the body may not explode. I was told of one woman who wished to establish her right to a rich man's property; consequently at the critical moment she dashed from the arms of her friends and with one blow of a stick

broke the head of her late liege lord, thus clearly
showing her heirship, as only the legal heir is
entitled to perform this last kind office for the
dear departed.

I heard one rather peculiar story while in India
in regard to the cremation of the dead. I sat
at dinner beside an English official who had been
many years in the Government service of India.
In the course of the conversation I asked him
what he thought about cremation. He said, with
a smile : " Well, I am perhaps a little preju-
diced in regard to the cremation of the dead.
I had rather a peculiar experience." I settled
back in my chair, hoping I was to hear one of
the many stories of Indian life which these old
officials have to tell us if they find we are interested in the lives of the people amongst whom
they work. He said : " I had an acquaintance
once, a Scotchman, who died here in India,
and asked in his will that I and another
friend would cremate him, and not allow an
Indian hand to touch him, but that we should
personally attend to all the details. We were
young then in things Indian, and made our first
mistake in buying the wood for the pyre. Un-
fortunately for our friend, the wily wood-
merchant sold us green wood, and for the first
day he only smoked. By the second day the
wood had dried out, and all would have been
well if we had known that the skull of a person
burned should be broken in order to allow the
gases to escape. We did not know this—our

friend blew up. We spent the remainder of the second day in gathering his remains and replacing them upon the fire. The third day the work was fully accomplished; his ashes were collected and now repose in a beautiful urn in his family chapel near Edinburgh."

Ceremonies are held and sacrifices are made for ten days by the members of a family in which there has been a death. If the deceased was a married man, it is on the tenth day that the widow is degraded into her state of widowhood. This rite is called "the cutting of the cord," because then the tali, the symbol of wifehood, is cut, and the woman has no more place in Hindu society. The relatives and friends come to the house and deck the poor woman in all her festive clothing; jewels are put upon her, flowers, and sandal-paste. Her friends mourn with her for a time, then her bright clothing is removed, her beautiful black hair is cut, and she must remain for ever close-shaven and clothed in a garment of white. She may attend no feast, is permitted to eat only one meal a day, and that should be prepared by her own hands, may not partake of meat, and if she is so unfortunate as to be poor in this world's goods she becomes the drudge and servant of her husband's family. She is considered unclean, a thing of ill-omen, so unlucky that if a man were starting on some business venture and on leaving his doorway should by chance meet a widow he would return to his house and say a few prayers to counteract his bad luck.

INDIAN WOMEN SPINNING.

To face p. 148.

When the widow is a child, not yet arrived at the age of living with her husband, the only ceremony at the death is the cutting of the tali cord. The other ceremonies and degradations are reserved for the time when she arrives at the full age of wifehood, when the whole ceremony is enacted as though the wife had been a real wife, and the little girl-widow is compelled to join that great army of women in India, nearly twenty million strong, of whom a million are child-widows.

I met a great many widows in India, and even among the Brahmo-Samaj, which sect is now trying to break the tyrannical yoke of custom, I never heard of one who dared to brave public opinion and remarry. I knew one charming widow—I think the most beautiful woman I saw in India—who had practically broken all class restrictions except this last. It was said that she had been in love with a man for many years, and he had repeatedly tried to persuade her to undergo the censure of her people by marrying him, but she dared not do it. She was only thirty years old, but she must remain until the end of her life a widow, almost an outcast.

In the cities and among the modernized people of India this state does not hold such sorrow for women as in the villages and country districts, where the people have not come into contact with Western civilization. In these purely Hindu towns, where all social life is controlled by custom and the influences of superstition and religion, when the woman can no longer wear the red mark of wifehood upon her forehead, her case is pitiable.

The Indian Government has made laws legalizing the remarriage of widows, but even when it has the Government sanction, custom and tradition are too strong, and practically no woman will take advantage of it. It would mean not only lifelong disgrace for her, but also would reflect so severely upon her relatives and the members of her caste that they would be involved in endless disgrace.

There are many homes scattered throughout India for these helpless women. Pundita Ramabai has a place near Poona where she has nearly eight hundred widows in her charge, and they are a sad sight as they go in squads of from two to three hundred to their work at the printing press or at the looms attached to the mission. Some widows had been with her for years, and quite likely will remain for life, as no one will marry a widow, and they do not seem to be acquiring a practical education with which they could earn their living in the world. The Gaekwar of Baroda is solving the widow question by educating them as teachers at the Government expense, only asking that in return for his care they devote a certain number of years as school-teachers in his State.

Pundita Ramabai's home for widows is a very remarkable institution, and well repays one for a visit. It is a faith mission—that is, its members

do not receive a salary, but depend upon dona-
tions for their support.   What remains after the
expenses of the establishment have been met is
divided among the workers according to their
needs.   They are a very devoted band, with an
orthodox, old-fashioned brand of religion that
holds the wrath of God and the terrors of hell
over these emotional women, whose only outlet
for their emotions is their prayers, and at noon
they are permitted to pray aloud and express
their desires and their states of feeling.   One
day we heard a great buzzing, sounding from
the distance like an immense swarm of bees,
and found it was the 1,350 widows, rescued street
women, and children having their noonday
prayer.   Some of them worked themselves into
a veritable ecstasy of religious emotion, swaying
their bodies, the tears running down their faces
as they prayed for the forgiveness of their sins,
real or imaginary.

The business manager was more interested in
the practical than the religious aspects of the
mission, and looked at the whole question with
the eye of the man who has to provide for all
these people who give nothing to the common
good.   When asked the outcome of it all, he
said he could not see what good was being
accomplished except in the actual saving of the
lives.   They could not marry, they could not
support themselves, they were helpless, and would
be a burden on others' shoulders so long as they
lived.   He said : " Now look !   There go four

hundred women who should be married to-
morrow; but who will marry them? No Hindu
would dare break his caste by marrying one of
them. It would completely ostracize him from
his community. And again, we would not want
to marry a Christian girl to a Hindu or a
Mohammedan."

I asked: "Are there no Christian boys to
marry them?"

He replied: "There are not enough to go
around, and even a Christian does not marry a
widow."

"Do you ever have any offers?" I asked.

He laughed. "Yes, once in a while some man
takes courage and comes here to find a wife,
but he generally goes away without one. We
seem here rather to go on the principle of getting
rid of the speckled apples first, and if there is
a girl with a hare lip, or only one eye, she is
the one trotted out for inspection. Naturally,
the boy beats a hasty retreat, saying he believes
he does not want to get married to-day."

The lot of the widowed woman in India is
not so pitiable if she has been so fortunate as
to have borne sons. In India, as in all Eastern
countries, filial piety, the respect for parents, is
bred into the very fibre of the man's soul. When
the mother becomes a widow and dons the gown
of white, her son cares for her and cherishes
her all her days. She is still the ruler of his
household, and it would be a most unfilial son,
on whom his world would soon cry shame, if

he did not ask the advice of his mother on
matters of importance, nor heed her warnings
in times of stress. Her whole life is given for
others, as this world is supposed to have no
joys for her except the joy of service. For
her " this world is but a dream : God alone is
real " ; and her days are passed in caring for
the many lives around her and in prayers and
religious rites that will help her to more swiftly
pass the time ere she may join her lost one.
The woman of India who has lost her mate turns
instinctively to the gods for solace, because she
has been taught from childhood that " the
religion of the wife lies in serving her husband :
the religion of the widow lies in serving God."

CHAPTER X

HYDERABAD AND THE MOHAMMEDAN WOMAN

THE city of Hyderabad seems to have been dropped to the earth from an Oriental dream. It is the most Eastern city in this most Eastern land, and you are filled with a sense that it is not at all real, but especially staged and set for your amusement, and when you leave, it will all disappear. The gaily painted shops will be pulled down and put in the property-room, the goldsmiths who make the bracelets, nose-rings, and necklaces for the pretty, dark-eyed women within the zenanas is only waiting for his cue to leave the stage. The men on the corners with their great wreaths of white flowers, with their marigolds and garlands to be hung about the necks of friends, or to curtain the doorways at some feast or wedding, are there only for show, to add colour to the picture. These women passing by with saris of purple or crimson, with gleaming bracelets and tinkling anklets, with kohl-blackened eyes that stare at you wonderingly from above the closely drawn sari, or, what is

A CARRIAGE FOR WOMEN.

To face p. 154.

more peculiar to visitors from the West, the
women draped in long white cloaks like winding-
sheets, which cover them completely from the
view of the passer by, seem part of the chorus ;
and the sheen of knives and guns and huge silver
chains hanging over the shoulder of the man from
the North, the elephant swaying slowly down the
street, looking with keen, twinkling eyes at the
people who make way for him, are all a part of
the pantomime, or a mirage caused by the
brilliant sunshine of this Southland.

We are told that Hyderabad is the oldest and
greatest native State in the Indian Empire, and
we have heard from childhood of the magnificence of the Nizam of Hyderabad, the man who
seemed to outrival Solomon with his palaces, his
jewels, and his wives. His hospitality was given
with Oriental lavishness. Those who were fortunate enough to be his guests at the great Durbar
at Delhi, when King George was proclaimed
Emperor of India, will never forget the gorgeous-
ness and prodigality of his entertainment. For
sixteen months he had an army of workmen clear-
ing the ground, making the lawns and flower-
gardens, and erecting the tents that were to
accommodate his guests and the four thousand
people he took with him from Hyderabad. His
women were lodged in an old palace at a distance
from the tents of the guests and were unseen,
viewing the spectacle from afar.

Even those of the immediate circle surround-
ing the Nizam at Hyderabad knew nothing of his

private life within the zenana, and only conjectures were made in regard to the number of women within its walls. Gossip says that when the late Nizam died there was a cartload of broken glass bracelets (the bangles that are worn by wives, but that are broken on their wrists when they become widows) taken away from the palace. This fortunate man was credited with a great many more wives than he actually possessed. Hyderabad is a feudal country, with many of the customs that prevailed in France under the old feudal régime. The Nizam is the overlord. His feudal princes when possessing a pretty daughter are always anxious to give her as wife to the Nizam. He perhaps may accept her and send her to his women's quarters, never seeing her again. But her people are satisfied, as they have the honour of having a daughter in the Imperial zenana, consequently a friend at Court, as she will naturally remember her family when Imperial offices or gifts are being distributed. She receives a stated income, said to range from sixty dollars to four hundred dollars a month, according to her status, number of children, etc.

The Nizam was planning to give his first ball while I was in Hyderabad, and every one was on the *qui vive* regarding those who should be asked and those who should not. It is remarkable how everything seems to revolve around the ruler of one of these principalities. His Highness is an absolute autocrat concerning the life and actions of his people, and the foreigners seem to have caught the infection, because in every State we visited the name of the ruler was on all tongues. " His Highness thinks so and so," or " His Highness does not think so and so," was the ultimate, final word for everything. His greatness and his Oriental splendour seem to overpower the people and make them subservient. Yet it is not from any personal contact, as few of even the Nizam's ministers have seen him, and his people never have that honour, unless at some great Durbar, where, arrayed in royal magnificence, he permits them to view him upon his throne, or when, as he is being swiftly whirled along in his motor, four shrill blasts from the whistles of the police notify the populace that their ruler is passing.

A native ruler seems to attract a genuine admiration and respect from his subjects. He appeals to their instincts with his display. They love to hear the glories of his magnificence, to see his elephants, his guards, and his foreign motors. He can understand his people and his people understand him ; and even if the taxes are oppressive and he grinds the faces of the people into the dust to get money to squander upon his favourites and to build great palaces, the peasant will bear it all and not complain, as he feels it is ordained, and his Rajah is the child of the gods and entitled to his very life.

There is no fear in the State of Hyderabad that the present race of rulers will become extinct. When a child is born to the Nizam there is a public holiday in the State, the schools are closed, cannon are fired, and every one is supposed to rejoice with the happy father. While we were there the people enjoyed four public holidays within eight days arising from this fact, and nine more were expected the following week.

While we were in this State there arose a case that was causing a great deal of comment. The son of a woman was killed and the murderer was condemned to death. In this Mohammedan country the law " a life for a life " prevails, and the death penalty cannot be revoked unless the heir of the dead man demands it. In some Hindu communities, where the saving of life is a meritorious performance, the village or city will often raise a certain sum and offer it to the heir in exchange for the life of the condemned prisoner. Men, I was told, will sometimes take the money, but women, especially if it was their son or husband who was killed, will practically always demand the life. In this instance the woman, who was a devout Mohammedan, took the money and sent it to help her fellow-Mohammedans in their war with the infidel Italians. Her religious zeal overcame the instinct for revenge, so deeply planted within the breast of all followers of the Arabian prophet.

At tea at the home of a Mohammedan I met several ladies, who willingly discussed with me the difference between the social customs of our Western land and those governing the life of the woman of the East. I was told that there is no society life as we know it, no calling, nor promiscuous making of new acquaintances. The social life centres around the three great events of Indian life—births, weddings, and deaths. If a wedding occurs in a family, the mother will send invitations to all the ladies of the same social standing as herself, and, dressed in their most gorgeous saris and jewels, they come to the house, where elaborate refreshments are served with much gossiping and merry-making. The guests stay hours or days, according to their relationship to the family. Also at times of death they go and offer their condolences to the bereaved family, and although colours are much more subdued at the time of sorrow than at the time of rejoicing, it is often another place in which to show off new finery. These secluded women feel like the little girl who stopped to see a friend on her way to a funeral. She was dressed in a bright pink sari, and when remonstrated with on wearing such a gay dress on such a mournful occasion, said, " Why, how can I be sure that I will get another chance to show it."

I said to my hostess in the course of the conversation : " If I were a Mohammedan or a Hindu lady and came here to live, would the ladies whose husbands perhaps had business associations with my husband come to call upon me ? " She said : " No, not at all. You would never meet the ladies unless at the time of some festivity you were invited." I asked the reason for this, and they answered, " Custom "—the word that rules the whole Eastern world. This lack of exchange of courtesies between new people is traced in some cases to the attitude of the husbands, who seem afraid to allow their wives to make new acquaintances. They must decide whom the wife shall visit. They must know that the house visited is strictly secluded, that the hostess has no advanced ideas, and that the husband is a man of standing before they allow their women to make new friends. They say that it is the desire of protection, not deprivation of liberty, that causes them to take such care of their dear ones.

An Englishwoman ten years ago tried to meet the Indian ladies, and sent sixty invitations for a tea. Only three of the invited guests put in an appearance. She persisted, convinced the husbands that no male eyes would gaze upon their secluded treasures, and now the original sixty have come with nearly every high-class lady in Hyderabad, so that on her reception days the house is crowded.

There is a club where the Mohammedan and Hindu ladies meet once a month and play badminton, and eat much cake and gossip. Still, they are not as yet taking any active interest in social work, nor in what is going on in the world outside. Mme. Sarojinni Naidu, the Indian poetess whose charming poems have been so well received in England, and who is herself a social favourite in that country, has been trying

to interest the ladies of Hyderabad in social
work among women. She has been specially
interested in reviving the old industry of silk-
weaving, and the weavers through her efforts
have been encouraged to do their best work.
She has sold thousands of rupees worth of the
beautiful silks to her friends within the zenanas,
but it is rather discouraging work, as it has caused
her to be looked upon with suspicion by many of
the officials, who fear that she may be using her
influence with the people for some Socialistic
movement.

While in Hyderabad I saw a great deal of
this wonderfully attractive woman, who looks like
a young girl, but who is the mother of children
nearly as big as herself. She herself is not
" purdah," and she has violated the customs of
her caste by marrying a man of another caste.
She goes to public entertainments and lives the
life of an Englishwoman. I went with her to
see the " sports," that form of entertainment
which always follow the English wherever they
go. They were held at the race track, and in the
grand stand were the entire foreign community,
with a mixture of Indian gentlemen. We
watched the riders in the field below, and I must
confess the Indian gentlemen easily carried the
honours. They are wonderful horsemen, and
are most picturesque. I think there is no hand-
somer man in the world than the high-class
Indian gentleman. With his clear brown skin,
his large black eyes, his stately carriage, and

11

magnificent physique, accentuated by the pugaree or turban on his head, he is a picture that, once seen, cannot easily be forgotten. The average Englishman looks either too fat or too thin, does not hold himself well, has generally, if a resident in the East, a most unhealthy complexion, and in comparison with his Indian neighbour makes a very poor showing.

Mme. Naidu was the only Indian woman in the grand stand, and after tea was served, she asked me if I would like to visit the Indian women. We went upstairs to an enclosed room, which was filled with Indian ladies, who could see all that was going on in the grounds below, but were protected from view by the carved woodwork enclosing the room. They came to a side entrance in their carriages or motors; a screen of canvas was made from their carriage to the entrance so that they could pass immediately from their carriage to a covered stairway, themselves unseen.

There were about twenty ladies, dressed in most brilliant colours and decked with an immense amount of jewellery. One woman had seven piercings in her ears, in four of which were set small buttons of turquoises, and in the others great hoops of gold in which were hanging pearls about the size of a pea. In her right nostril was a diamond and in her left a ruby. Her arms were covered with bracelets, and there were five necklaces of diamonds around her neck. Her trousers, the ugly trousers of the Mohammedan lady, were of bright pink brocade, the tunic was of white, and over it all was a long veil of light blue gauze.   One would imagine a glaring clash of colours, but all this riot of colour blends and makes the right setting for the dark beauty of these Indian women.   They are extremely pretty, with the colouring of an Italian or Spaniard from the South ; their big black eyes are shaded by long silky lashes, their noses are most delicate, and they have exquisitely shaped mouths.   I do not think that I saw an ugly woman all the time I was visiting the " purdah " women of India.   Some of them with age become a little too stout, but their dress disguises the figure if too well blessed with flesh, and softens harsh outlines if too thin.

The women in this secluded enclosure seemed to be enjoying themselves much more than the conventional Englishwomen below them.   There was a table with a varied assortment of non-alcholic drinks, and many kinds of cakes and sweets.   Each lady had her silver pan-box, and made pan for her friends, all chatting and laughing with the utmost freedom and good-fellowship.   They do not seem to feel it a deprivation at all to be compelled to pass their lives with women.   I am sure they would feel very ill at ease if they thought that they could be seen by any man except their husband, brother, or immediate relative.

I had an example of what instinct will do in the fear of being seen by some one outside of the family circle.   Mme. Naidu and I called upon a Mohammedan lady who was strictly " purdah." We were taken into a drawing-room furnished in European fashion, where the father-in-law of our hostess was chatting with another gentleman.   The stranger left immediately, but the father-in-law remained to talk with me while Mme. Naidu went in search of the mistress of the house.   She returned soon, and said to the man, " You must leave," and after his departure the lady entered.   When she sat down she noticed that one of the blinds of the window was open, and she drew her sari across her face and spoke to Mme. Naidu, who went to the window and closed the blind.   Even that did not satisfy her, and a servant was called, who saw that all the windows were securely closed and that no one could possibly look into the room from the outside.   It seemed a useless precaution to me, as the windows opened on to a garden, and no one could pass unless some member of the household. She laughed apologetically and said : " I know what you think, but I cannot sit here with any degree of comfort if I think some one, a servant or one of my husband's guests, might pass by. It is instinct ; my mother and my mother's mother were ' purdah ' women, and it is in the blood."

She asked us to come to her rooms and look at some new clothing.   Her rooms were big and rather bare, as are most rooms in this hot country, but the furniture was all European.   Bed, dress-

ing-table, and chairs all looked as if made in
England or France.   She had a servant bring
her pan-box.   This giving of pan is the first
thing offered to a guest on arrival and the
last thing on going away.   Her pan-box was
of silver, about nine inches wide by twelve long.
It had a shallow tray in the top, in which was
kept in tiny compartments the betel-nut and
spices.   In the bottom of the box, covered with
a damp cloth, were the leaves.   The hostess takes
a leaf, covers it with a thin layer of lime, and with
a pair of scissors breaks a betel-nut into small
pieces, puts it with half a dozen different spices
into the leaf, folds it up, sticking a clove through
the leaf as a fastener, and hands it to the guest.
The guest removes the clove and places the leaf
in the mouth, where it makes a huge bunch on
the side of the face until it is slowly masticated.
It gives forth a juice which colours the inside
of the mouth and the teeth a dark red, but not
permanently, as it rinses quite easily.   The
pan has a spicy taste, and leaves the mouth
feeling deliciously clean, I presume owing to the
lime in it.   Many of the great houses have a
servant or slave whose only duty is to make
pan for the inmates of the zenana.   One such
servant said she made five hundred a day and
her wrist became quite lame from time to time
caused by cutting the betel-nut.
    Our hostess had a box of clothing put in front
of her on the floor, and she showed us a beautiful
collection of saris of woven gold cloth made in

Benares, long tunics of embroidered chiffon-like gauze, and trousers of heavy gold and silver goods, almost like tapestry.

I asked them to tell me the duties of a high-class lady of Hyderabad.   Mme. Naidu laughed and said—

" About eight o'clock in the morning my lady yawns, and a slave-girl will say, ' Will not the Begum rise?' and the Begum will slowly get out of bed and allow her slave to brush her teeth with powdered charcoal and wash her face and hands. Then she would sit down upon a mat and have her hair dressed, while other slaves came in with articles of dress or of the toilet.   Soon the other women of the household would join her, and they would chew betel-nut and talk and gossip until about ten o'clock, when a large tray would be brought in with breakfast, consisting of rice and curry and sweets.   After breakfast, more friends or relatives come in, and the sewing women and higher servants, and they all talk and laugh together.   In the afternoon the silk merchants may send their wares or the jewellers their bracelets and rings and precious stones, which are brought into the zenana by women. These shopwomen are great gossips, and tell all the news from other zenanas—who is engaged and who married and what presents were given, etc.   The women shop and haggle, and perhaps buy and perhaps do not, and by the time the merchants leave it is time to eat again.   In the evening the husband or the sons visit the women's

quarters and brings the Begum the news of the
world of men outside, and then it is time to
sleep again."

A great many women—nearly all Indian
women, in fact—attend personally to their households. For instance, I went with one of my
friends, who belonged to a very rich and powerful
family, to call upon her mother, and found her
and her daughter-in-law sitting in the courtyard
preparing the vegetables for dinner. All ladies
know how to cook, and think it no disgrace to
prepare the dinner with their own hands. If a
guest is to be especially honoured, the mother or
wife will prepare the meal for him. In a Hindu
community, where the food must be cooked by
a person of their own or a higher caste, where
no one of a lower caste is even allowed to look
into the kitchen, it might cause great annoyance
if the women of the household did not know how
to cook, as even in India the mistress has the
servant question with which to contend from time
to time.

In these old families in Hyderabad there are a
great many people under the one roof. The
patriarchal family life prevails—that is, the sons
bring their wives to their father's home, and a
large house shelters many families. The mother
is the head of the women's quarters and her word
is law. Innumerable servants and poor relations are ever present, and to our Western eyes
disorder and chaos seem to reign. There are
some old families in this city that keep up the

state of princes or petty kings. There is one great lady who is surrounded by a bodyguard of amazons, women dressed as soldiers, who salute and present arms with military precision when her courtyard is entered by a visitor.

We went from the house of our young hostess, loaded down with pan and fruit, to the home of a colonel in the Nizam's bodyguard. His wife is " purdah," but his daughter is allowed to be seen in public. In the drawing-room was a man tuning the piano, and Mme. Naidu said to the daughter, " Your mother cannot come here. There is a man." The daughter replied : " Oh, it is all right, he is blind." The mother had travelled extensively in Europe, Egypt, and Turkey. While abroad she went about freely as any European, only becoming the secluded Indian wife while in her own country. Her daughter was to be married and she showed me the clothes for the trousseau. There were about fifty complete outfits, made of gorgeous Benares cloth, heavy with gold. This clothing lasts a lifetime, and is handed down from daughter to daughter, as styles do not radically change. The mother told me that the custom of giving so much clothing is dying out, and money is given instead, allowing the daughter to buy from time to time, according to her fancy.

While we were talking the husband came in. He was dressed in English riding clothes, and was a very up-to-date man-of-the-world. The moment he entered, the mother and daughter, who up to this time had been chatting affably and freely, became silent. They virtually did not speak a word while he was in the room, but became at once true Indian women, silent before that superior being—the man.

CHAPTER XI

MOHAMMEDANISM WITHIN THE ZENANA

WE are often told that Mohammedan women are not religious, that they leave all devotional exercises for their lords and masters, who are accountable to Allah for their salvation, and to whom they must look for permission to enter the abode of the blessed. It is a fact that the women followers of the Arabian prophet are not seen in the mosques, because no Mohammedan woman appears in a public place where she may come in contact with the other sex. Mohammed discouraged the worship of women in public by saying, " The presence of women in the mosques inspires men with feelings other than those purely devotional."

Although restricted to the home in which to say her prayers, the Mohammedan woman is very religious, and often more narrow and bigoted than her husband, who has the opportunity of broadening his religious views by contact with those of other faiths. The Mohammedan religion, like those of Western lands, has its

MOHAMMEDAN WOMEN, HYDERABAD.

To face p. 170.

divisions and subdivisions, differing from each other on the subject of ritualism and the different interpretations of the Koran. The two most important branches of El Islam are the Shiahs and the Sunnis. At the death of the prophet, Abu Bekr was elected to take his place—wrongfully, as many believe. They feel that the mantle of prophethood should have fallen upon the shoulders of his son-in-law, Ali, who was one of his first disciples and his cousin. The coterie who adhered to the election of the caliph instead of the hereditary descent are called the Sunnis. All of the Egyptians, the Turks, and many Indians are followers of this party. Those who think that Ali was deprived of his just rights are called the Shiahs; the Persians, many Arabs, and a few Indians compose the main body of this division. Ali was finally made caliph, but was murdered, the caliphate passing out of his family instead of descending to his grandsons, Hossain and Hassan, who rebelled against the ruling caliph and were killed in battle. They are considered the great martyrs of the Mohammedan faith, and their deaths are mourned annually by the Shiahs.

We were in Hyderabad, the great Mohammedan State of India, at the time of mourning, and I was fortunate enough to be asked to a "mourning party," given by the women of one of the old Mohammedan families. It was most exceptional, as outsiders are never asked to these homes during this time of religious emotion.

Even their Sunni friends and their acquaintances in the Hindu faith, know that intruders are not looked upon kindly during the days set apart for sorrow.

We arrived at the home, which was surrounded by a great wall, in which was a massive wooden door studded with iron nails. In the olden time these homes were used as fortresses, and were made strong enough to repel an invasion by the enemy. Within an embrasure by the side of the gate was a man on guard, with a gun beside him. It is true that the gun was of an obsolete pattern, that would quite likely do the user more damage than any one else, if the guard had been called upon to act, but it looked picturesque. The guard immediately turned his back when he saw that the carriage contained ladies, and our servant went ahead to see that all men-servants were out of sight before my Mohammedan friends would enter the courtyard. We drove into what seemed an immense stable-yard. Bullocks were standing by the side of great lumbering carts, horses were in their stalls, and stable accessories were scattered about in great disorder. A curtain was raised by a woman-servant, disclosing a short stone stairway, ascending which we found ourselves in the women's quarters. It was a courtyard, with rooms opening upon it from the four sides. These rooms were more like large alcoves, being separated from the court only by arches.

At one end was a large room, where about sixty ladies were sitting on the floor in front of a strip of white cloth, that served as table and tablecloth combined. They were seated on the three sides of the room, leaving the open space in the middle for the servants to pass while serving the food. We left our shoes at the entrance and were taken to a servant, who poured water over our hands from a brass ewer, allowing it to fall into a basin in which was some finely chopped straw to conceal the water. Our hostess seated us opposite her, and an old servant dipped from a central bowl of rice a generous helping for me, and then various curries, unknown to me, were passed. I watched my friend, and took from the dishes she favoured, mixing it with the rice upon my plate, making rather a sticky mess, that was conveyed to my mouth with difficulty. Eating with the fingers is not so easy as it may appear to a casual observer, but evidently practice makes perfect, because all seemed most adept, using only the thumb and three fingers of the right hand. No food must be touched with the left hand, as it is, religiously, unclean.

After my feet had so thoroughly gone to sleep that they ceased from paining me, I took the opportunity of looking around and trying to become acquainted with my neighbours. The ladies wore no jewellery, and their dresses were supposed to be of a subdued hue, yet every colour of the rainbow was represented except red, which is the colour of joy and associated with festive occasions. The Mohammedan dress is not so graceful as is the Indian sari. The women wear a pair of tight trousers, made of satin, silk, or brocade, coming to the tops of their embroidered slippers. Over the chest is a small sleeveless jacket, then a tunic of white or embroidered gauze, and over all a chiffon-like drapery which is drawn over the head. All of these outer draperies were of so diaphanous a material that they did not disguise the outlines of the figure.

Down the centre of the strips of cloth which served as table were great dishes of rice and sweets, many curries, fruits, and an elaborate assortment of cakes. Servants were everywhere, and it was hard for a stranger to distinguish between some of the servants and their mistresses, as many of the former were very well dressed and covered with jewellery. They wore brace-lets, anklets, nose-rings, ear-rings, and necklaces, mainly of silver or glass ; but one often saw the glint of gold upon the neck of a serving-woman, and found she was the personal slave of some member of the family.

Slavery exists still in Hyderabad, although in a modified form. No person of good family would think of selling a slave, and the slaves themselves feel the honour of belonging to one of the old families. In a quarrel with a servant a slave will draw herself up proudly and say, " You are only a servant—*I* belong to the family."

Both servants and slaves are treated with a familiarity unknown in the West. They take part in the conversation, enter the rooms without knocking—in fact, I don't believe there is such a thing as a locked door in all India—and talk to the mistress on terms of equality. While at dinner a small boy, very prettily dressed, came to the hostess and snuggled his head against her, while he stared at the peculiar-looking foreign woman opposite. I asked if he was her son. She turned his face up to study it more carefully, then said, " No ; he is the son of one of my sister's slaves."

Resisting all the importunities of my hostess to have my plate refilled with the curry and rice, we rose and went again to the servants in charge of the ewer and basin, and our hands were washed. We then adjourned to a courtyard, where many of the guests had preceded us. There appears to be no etiquette in regard to leaving the table ; when a guest has eaten her dinner she rises and leaves, not asking to be excused, nor feeling that it is necessary to wait for her hostess.

The ladies were sitting on the floor of the alcoves in groups of six or seven, and pan boxes were much in evidence. Our hostess went into the open courtyard and mounted a low, square table, over which was thrown a rug. We sat down opposite her and she proceeded to make pan for us, and we remained there for perhaps half an hour, waiting for the servants to

finish their dinner.   There were at least fifty
servants and slaves, all running around aimlessly,
doing whatever they found to do at the time,
with what seemed no system nor order governing
their work.   The mistress had rather a shrill
voice, and her orders could be heard very distinctly as she called to some one in another part
of the court.   I asked my friend if Indian ladies
generally had such loud voices and commanding
tones, and she laughed and said : " Well, if they
have not to begin with they soon acquire them,
as they must be heard above the confusion always
reigning in one of these great houses, where
there are innumerable servants, slaves, and
poor relations.   It takes a strong-minded
woman, and one with no mean executive ability,
to keep peace and harmony in an Eastern
zenana."

After every one had gossiped to her heart's
content, we went to a large room at the end of
the courtyard, which was fitted up as a chapel.
In front of an altar were three pieces of wood
wreathed with flowers to represent the tombs of
Ali, Hossain, and Hassan.   Facing the tombs
were ten girls, and the guests grouped themselves
around them on the floor.   When we were all
seated they began to chant.   One would sing
a line, then the rest would join their voices and
sing four or five lines ; then a short pause, and
the leader would again start the chant.   The
listeners were absolutely quiet, and the music
rose and fell in weird, minor strains that sounded

tragic even to ears that could not understand the words. The whole story of the slaying of the martyrs was told, and this recital of their passion play moved the hearers deeply. From one part of the room I heard a sob, then from another, and soon there was not a dry eye in the place. At a certain strain in the music all rose, preceded by the women carrying the miniature tombs, and marched slowly into an outer courtyard, where incense was waved over the flower-wreathed pieces of wood, after which a return was made to the room and the chanting commenced again. We did not sit down, and the most dramatic part of the performance began. All stood and beat their breasts in time with the music, and, as chorus to the verses, would cry, " Hossain, Hassan ! Hossain, Hassan ! " The servants beat their breasts so severely that it seemed they would seriously hurt themselves, and it is considered a great mark of piety to severely chastise themselves at this time, but the ladies were more conservative and kept time with light taps.

This continued, with slight intermissions, for half an hour, some sobbing, others crying quietly. At the end each one dropped to her knees with her face towards Mecca, and from outside the wall the voice of a man from the mosque chanted a benediction. It was most exquisitely sung, and added the final touch to a weirdly beautiful scene—the moon shining down into the courtyard, the flickering lights before the tiny flower-

12

wreathed tombs, the dark-faced women in their pretty gowns, with the tears glistening on their eyelashes, kneeling, while the unseen voice cried softly, " Salaam! Peace be with you! There is no God but God."

HUSKING RICE IN A BURMESE VILLAGE.

To face p. 210

CHAPTER XII

BURMAH

PASSING from India to Burmah is in many ways like going from darkness to sunlight, from tears to gaiety. India is a land of tragedy; Burmah is a land of comedy. In India you see faces sad, worried, harassed, and life seems a bitter struggle for the great masses in their endeavour to keep the hungry wolf from the door. But in Burmah you are greeted with smiles, no one is serious, and no one except the Chinese seem to be really working. The women in the little booths within the bazaars, smoking their long cheroots, gossiping with their neighbours, and flirting with the youth passing by, give one the impression that it is not business in which they are interested, but that they are there for their amusement and to pass a few hours with their friends.

The dress also shows the difference in the temperaments of the people. In India the women's saris are made of dark reds, dark blues, and heavy purples. In Burmah the colours are light and gay; you rarely see a darkly clad person. The long piece of silk wound tightly around the woman's body is always of light blue, or pink, or yellow, or else a gay check composed of all three colours. The loose cotton or linen jacket is spotlessly white, and around the neck is thrown carelessly a piece of silk or a handkerchief of contrasting colour to the skirt. The hair, of ebony blackness, is well oiled and twisted high upon the head and twined with flowers. Their toes are tucked into small heelless slippers, which take a certain amount of dexterity to keep in place ; but all young girls learn early in life to give that flirtatious outward jerk of the heels which keep the slipper from falling, and also prevents the folds of the skirt from opening in front. The city belle when she starts forth upon the street has well powdered her nose and often touched her lips with carmine, and goes forth boldly to claim the admiration of all, not like the Indian woman, who is compelled to hide her charms behind the sari.

The man of Burmah also dresses in gaily coloured silks. He wears a long silk cloth around his body, tucks it in with a twist in front, and the remaining portion he allows to hang in folds or throws jauntily over his shoulder. He wears a short white cotton jacket, over which another one of darker cloth is worn for street wear. The old and wealthy when they are paying visits of ceremony or going to worship at the pagoda wear long white coats, closed only at the neck and reaching to the knee. Men of

BURMESE GIRL.

To face p. 180.

all classes wear flowered silk handkerchiefs around their heads as turbans, but when age comes these are exchanged for simple ones of white muslin.

The women of Burmah have unlimited freedom as compared with the women of other Eastern countries. Unlike the women of India, China, or Egypt, they, may, choose their own husbands and have a courtship such as we of the Western world so thoroughly understand. From the time of the first great event in a young girl's life, the boring of her ears, which announces to her world that she is no longer a child but a woman, until her betrothal, the Burmese girl looks forward to the finding of a husband as the one aim of her life. Until her ears are bored she is a child and may run and play with her brothers upon the village street, but finally the day, arrives when her friends and relatives bring with them the ear-borer and the soothsayer, and the frightened girl must pay, the price of gaining maidenhood. Her cries are drowned by the music and the talk and laughter that seem so heartless; but the pain is soon over, and she herself will make the hole larger by every, means in her power, because until the hole is large enough to receive the great round tube, nearly half an inch in diameter, she does not feel that she is indeed a woman. It is her initiation into womanhood, it corresponds to the entrance into the monastery or the tattooing of his legs of her brother, the sign that he is no longer a boy, but may sit with men and chew betel-nut and discuss affairs of the world with wondrous wisdom.

After the ear-boring ceremony each man our maiden sees may be a possible husband, and she copies the coquettish sway of the hips that is so effective in her older sister as she walks down the street with mother, aunt, or married friend, who carefully guards her from all improprieties now that she has arrived at marriageable age.

When all these arts have had the desired effect and her roving eye has alighted upon the man of her choice, the Burmese girl may have her days of courtship. She can meet her sweetheart at pwés, those festive parties that seem to occur every night in Burmah, at which she may have a stall for selling tobacco, or long cheroots, or flowers. This keeping of a stall is not lowering to a woman's social status, and numbers of well-to-do women set them up at all places where crowds are liable to congregate. There may be a reason for this besides the economic one, as it is said a stall or shop or booth within the bazaar is the quickest way of attracting a desirable husband. In the smaller towns there is scarcely a house where the women have not arranged a small shop for sale of betel-nut, coco-nuts, little looking-glasses, toilet articles, or cotton goods from Manchester. The profits of this little trade are given as pin-money to the wife or daughters. The English say that the Burmese woman is a better business

DANCING AT A VILLAGE FESTIVAL, BURMAH.

To face p. 183.

man than her husband, and that in driving a
sharp bargain her successes are far in advance
of those of her less aggressive husband.

Pagoda feasts offer exceptional opportunities
for lovelorn swains, and many young couples
have found their future happiness when gazing
into Buddha's eyes. Evening-time is courting-
time in all the world, especially in this country,
which is too hot during the day to permit of
any useless expenditure of energy, even by an
ardent lover. They also say that the men of
Burmah are influenced by the proverb that says:
" In the morning women are cross and peevish,
in the middle of the day they are testy and
quarrelsome, but at night they are sweet and
amiable."

If the lover does not expect to meet his sweetheart at a festival or a theatrical entertainment,
he waits around until he thinks the old people
have retired for the night, and then with a friend
or two as chaperons he calls upon his adored
one, and finds her with powdered face and pretty
dress awaiting him in the moonlit veranda. There
is little privacy in this courtship, because divisions
between the rooms are often only made of
matting, and mothers in Burmah are proverbial
for the quickness of hearing when it concerns
the courtship of their daughters. There is no
lovemaking as we know it—kissing, and holding of hands, and embracing—which would be
most shocking to the modest instincts of the
Burmese maiden. Yet love has signs, and finally

father's and mother's consent is asked, the dowry fixed, and the astrologer consulted, who will tell them if a boy born on Monday, and a girl on Wednesday may, wed.   No matter how ardently the match is desired by the interested parties, some unions, judged according to their birthdays, would be most unlucky.   For example :—

> Friday's daughter
> Didn't oughter
> Marry with a Monday's son;
> Should she do it
> Both will rue it,
> Life's last lap will soon be run.

Each day of the week is guarded by an animal, and it naturally follows that if a man was born on a day that was ruled by a serpent and a woman on a day ruled by a mongoose, the serpent's deadly enemy, they would surely not live happily together.   But if the parent's consent is given, the combination of birthdays are lucky, the dowry is satisfactory to all concerned, then the propitious day must be found from the horoscope for the actual wedding to take place. During June, July, August, and September, the Buddhist Lent, all marriages are barred to the strict followers of Buddha, and it would be a very unregenerate son or daughter who would shock his old father and mother by daring to ask to marry during this time.   Marriage is a very precarious proceeding, because if it takes place in certain months the couple will be rich, in other months they will always love each other, while there are unfortunate months that bring sickness and death to those tempting Hymen at this time. Nevertheless, notwithstanding all the obstacles that seem to be placed in the way of marriage, there are few spinsters in Burmah, and virtually every man over twenty years of age has a wife.

The marriage ceremony is a strictly civil affair, no religious rite entering into the performance. The friends meet at the house of the bride's parents, where a great feast has been prepared at the expense of the bridegroom's father, and the eating and drinking and publicity of the affair make the marriage as binding as are any marriages in Burmah. Contrary to all Eastern usages, the young couple take up their abode with the bride's parents instead of going to the home of the groom's people, which is the custom in India, China, and Japan. If the home roof is too small to shelter the new family, they may build a new home for themselves. This is not an expensive affair, as the houses are extremely simple. They are practically all of one story, because of the Burman's aversion to any one walking over his head. The house is built on posts, thus raising the floor seven or eight feet from the ground, which is very desirable in rainy weather. It consists of two or three rooms and an open balcony, where the family may sit of an evening or where the daughter of the house may receive her lover, and not interrupt the slumbers of father and mother, who have spread their sleeping-mats upon the floor of the main living-room.

In the rainy season the cooking is done in one of the rooms, but in the long, dry months the yard at the back of the house serves as kitchen. In the smaller towns the roofs are thatched with palm-leaves or with grass, but in the cities the ugly iron roofs are now seen, with here and there a more pretentious roof of tiling.

Moving is not a laborious process, as there is little necessary furniture in a Burmese home. A few rush mats, which serve for beds, some rugs and blankets for use when nights are cold, which during the day are rolled up and placed in an unused corner of the room, a cooking-range, which is simply a square box filled with earth on which the wood is lighted, some earthen pots for making curries and the cooking of the rice, a water-jar, ladles made of the half of a coco-nut placed on a handle, the huge round lacquer tray, which serves as table, and the bowls for the curries and deserts.

With nearly every house there is a small yard, in which are found flowers if the wife is inclined to love the beautiful; but if she is more practically inclined chickens hold sway within the small domain, until the evil day arrives for them when they pass into the curry-pot. The strict Buddhist does not utilize the eggs, believing that they hold the germ of life which it would be sinful to destroy. These Burmese roosters can take the place of clocks, as it is said that they crow regularly four times a day—at sunrise, noon, sundown, and at midnight. The story goes that in the olden time there was a great fire made of books that contained unlawful teaching. Among these books were those of a famous astrologer, and after the fire the cocks came and ate the ashes, thus taking into their very being the knowledge of the stars and the actions of the sun.

If the wife lives in the city, she does not have the weary task of husking the rice, as it is bought ready for cooking, nor does she need waste much thought in planning the menu for the day. The two meals are practically the same—the plain boiled rice upon the table-tray, around which sit the household, squatting upon their heels. No knives or forks are needed, as each takes upon his plate from the central dish the rice, pours over it curry, arranges on the top the vegetables and condiments that he loves, and eats it with the forks with which Nature has provided him—his fingers. The food is very good if too much dried fish, which is a delicacy loved by Burmans, or garlic has not been incorporated in the curries. Only water is drunk at mealtime. If the husband has acquired the habit of tippling, which has come to Burmah with other foreign customs, he must go to the shop where it is sold to indulge in what, to every good householder, is still a thing of which to be ashamed.

After meals every one smokes—father, mother,

and children. It is said that baby learns while at his mother's breast to take the long cigar from between her lips and puff it between alternate draughts at Nature's font ; but Burmese deny this most indignantly, and say that smoking is forbidden the children until they have learned to walk. I can quite believe this, because it would take a strong baby to manage the enormous cheroot smoked by all Burmans, although they are so mild that they would not affect the nerves even of a child. The cigar seen in the homes is from six to eight inches in length and about an inch in diameter. It is made of the pith of a plant mixed with chopped tobacco-leaves, wrapped in the leaf of the teak-tree, the ends tucked in and tied by a piece of red silk, where stiff pieces of pith keep the loose tobacco from the mouth. It splutters and scatters its fine fire in all directions, and cannot be smoked by an amateur without danger to himself and all about him. These are often made within the home by the wife and daughters, yet they may be seen in tiny booths at all festivities, where pretty girls sell them to admiring swains who are too lazy to roll them for themselves.

Chewing betel-nut is also indulged in by both man and wife, and the stain it leaves upon the lips and tongue is not an addition to the beauty of the mouth ; yet it can be easily cleansed, as witness the pretty teeth and rosy lips of the women one meets in the street. There is no furniture to dust, few dishes to wash, and little clothing to be sewn, and small care expended upon the children. Their daily bath consists in throwing a few buckets of water over their naked bodies, which they learn early to do for themselves, and often around a village well the tiny babies, dressed in only an amulet string, may be seen with coco-nut ladle throwing the cooling water over their bodies and shrieking with delight. The children of the poor go naked until about eight or nine years old, and those of the better class dress practically as do their fathers and mothers while in the street, although, even in houses of the rich, clothing is considered a useless luxury for the young.

The simple life leaves much time for the wife, which she employs in gossiping with friends, in attending pagoda festivals and pwés until that happy event arrives, the birth of the first child. From the moment it is known that the wife is to become a mother she is the recipient of much care and attention and presents from her family and from her friends, and when she can say, " I am the mother of a son," then, like all Oriental women, she has attained the great crown of womanhood. But because of the lack of medical skill in Burmah she has to face a most dreadful ordeal. As soon as her child is born the mother is rubbed all over with saffron, a fire lighted near her, and all the blankets that can be begged or borrowed are heaped upon her. She is given a drink prepared by the midwife for the purpose of making her perspire. This is given her many times a day, and together with the large bricks that are heated and wrapped in damp cloths and placed in her bed conspire to have the desired effect, and the poor mother passes seven days in a Turkish bath. Then on the seventh day, as a finish to this trying ordeal which she has undergone, she is forced to go through a most elaborate steaming process, and if this does not smother her completely, she is pronounced well. The midwife receives her mats, her allotment of rice and her shilling, and the woman returns to her household duties. In the larger towns now the Burmese woman may call in the European-trained doctor, and there are hospitals which answer the great need that the women have for proper care at this critical time of their lives. Yet I am told that the mortality at child-bearing is not so great as that in India and other Eastern countries. The main effect upon the woman is to age her greatly; at the birth of her first child she changes from the pretty girl-wife to the middle-aged woman.

About two weeks after the birth of the child a great feast is given to celebrate the naming of the new arrival, and on this day also the young man's head is washed for the first time. All the friends of the family and the neighbours are invited, and they come, bringing presents with them to help pay for the feast. The mother sits down with her child in her arms, then some elder or relation of the parents suggests the name, and everybody accepts it at once, whereupon all adjourn to the feast, where they eat, chew betel, and smoke cheroots until nightfall. If the people have sufficient means, there is a pwé, which lasts until morning.

It is a rule amongst families that a child's name must begin with one of the letters belonging to the day on which it was born, and they all believe that the stars which were in evidence at the hour of birth decide a man's character. A man born on Monday will be jealous, on Tuesday honest, on Wednesday bad-tempered, on Thursday quiet, on Friday garrulous, on Saturday quarrelsome, and on Sunday stingy. Each day also has a particular animal which represents it. Monday is represented by a tiger, Tuesday, a lion, etc., and in temples one sees yellow and wax candles made in the form of these animals, representing his birthday, placed before the god by the man who wishes special benefits from lord Buddha.

Swinging by a couple of ropes from the roof is a rude home-made basket, which is used for baby's cradle. Even this useful article of furniture in which the Burmese baby passes his sleeping hours is subject to the actions of belligerent spirits, and must be hung in such a manner as not to tempt the nats to use it for a resting-place. Burmese mothers, like mothers all over the world, croon lullabies to their babies as they swing them back and forth while waiting for the sand-man to come. I give a verse

of one of the popular lullabies known generally
to all babies in Burmah—

> Nasty, naughty, noisy baby,
> If the cat won't, nats will maybe
> Come and pinch and punch and rend you—
> If they do I won't defend you.
>> Oh, now please,
>> Do not tease,
>> Do be good,
>> As babies should,
> Just one tiny little while;
> Try to sleep, or try to smile.

When the son is eight or nine years of age
he goes as a matter of course to the monastery
school, which is open to all alike, the poor and
rich, and which is practically the only thing that
the priests, which flood this country, afford the
people in return for the food which is placed
in their begging-bowls each day. Every
Buddhist boy is taught to read and write, and
he learns many of the formulas connected with
the tenets of his religion and the stories relating
to the existence and teachings of Buddha. Until
the English came, all little boys went to the
monastery schools, but now there are Government
schools and Burmese laymen schools and many
private schools, to which the more advanced
Burmans are sending their sons; yet the school-
rooms in the monasteries are not vacant. The
young Burmese are not so forced by the economic
conditions to acquire the foreign education as
is the Indian boy, where life is much more diffi-

cult and the Government certificate simply a means to an end—Government employment. Until lately it was not thought necessary to educate the girls. To be pretty, to know how to take care of her household, to smile sweetly, and be of a gay disposition were sufficient for a woman ; and as book knowledge would not help her in those accomplishments, book knowledge was, therefore, dispensed with. But now the larger towns provide educational facilities for girls, and in Rangoon and Mandalay there are many private schools for the daughters of the better class.

Until a Buddhist has entered the monastery, joining the noble order of the yellow robe, if for no longer than a day, he is nothing more than a mere animal. He has a name given him for worldly purposes, so has a dog, a horse, or a cow ; but until he has shown himself ready to leave the world by retiring into the quiet and peace of the monasteries, he cannot expect to reap the good that he has sown in the past life, nor would it be possible for him to look forward to a happy future. At the beginning of the Buddhist Lent, all Buddhist boys from the age of twelve to fifteen don the yellow robe and carry the begging-bowl before the priest on his daily rounds. On this most important day in his life his parents give a feast, where the young novice, dressed in finest clothes, loaded with all the family jewels, goes slowly through the village, preceded by a band of music and

13

his friends and relatives dressed in their gayest clothing. He calls at the houses of his friends and pays respects to the officials of his village. Returning to his home, he finds, seated upon a raised daïs, several priests from the monastery to which he is soon to retire. They hold before their faces the large lotus-leafed-shaped fans, so as not to see the row of pretty women, dressed in their pinks and blues and yellows, flowers in their hair, jewels and chains on necks, and bracelets on arms, and pearl powder softening smiling faces. The solemnity of the ceremony commences when the boy throws off his fine clothing, and, binding a piece of white cloth around his loins, sits down before the barber and permits that glory of his boyhood, his long black hair, to be cut off close to his head. After he has been carefully shaved, water is poured over his body, and, dressed again in his bright clothing, he prostrates himself three times before the monks, begging in Pali, which quite likely he does not understand, that he may be admitted to the holy assembly. Then the yellow garments are given him, the begging-bowl is hung around his neck, and he is formally a member of the monastery. With the departure of the priests and the novice feasting begins, which, according to many Burmese festivities, lasts until dawn.

In many cases, if the boy is working and his services are needed, he remains in the monastery only long enough to enable him to go once around the village begging from door to door in

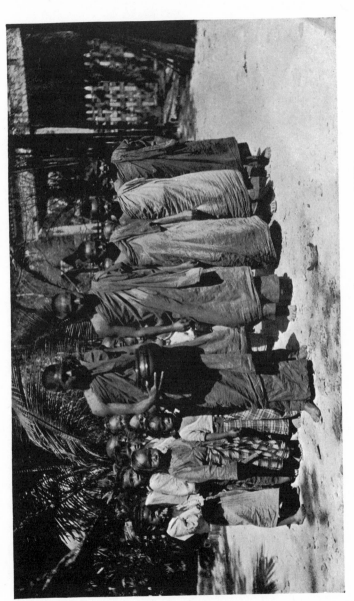

A BUDDHIST SCHOOL, MANDALAY (SHOWING BEGGING BOWL).

To face p. 194.

the train of the priests. Some stay seven days, some a fortnight, and others, if they are able, remain throughout the four months of Lent. Of course many of them enter the monastery for life, and there is no country in the world where there are so many priests as in Burmah. The monasteries offer a refuge for men in trouble, for those who desire to leave the cares of the world and lead a life of meditation and repose. And it is said that this departure from the world is made by many a man in this country, where women are noted for the strength of their characters and the length of their tongues.

The Burmese boy does not consider he has attained manhood until he has been tattooed. When I was first in Burmah, being rather near-sighted, I thought all Burmese men of the lower class wore short, dark, skin-tight drawers, but when I became more courageous and examined them more closely I found what I considered underclothing was the man's own skin. This had been tattooed from the waistline down to the kneecap with a series of pictures so closely set together that they could not be distinguished one from the other, and melted into a back-ground of blue and black, with here and there a softened red to accentuate the fading colours of the darker dye. This is a sign of manhood, which, the Burmese say, will probably not die out, because a Burman would be as ashamed to have a spotless white skin without a mark of the tattooer's needle as would the American boy to find no manly hairs upon his chin at the age when other boys begin to shave. And woe to the hapless youth if a wind-blown paso should show the girl he was courting a white and spotless leg ; she would tell him that his place was in the women's quarters and offer him a woman's dress ! Each figure in this mosaic has a meaning, and there are charms for protection of the body, for the gaining of a loved one, thus assuring the wearer great riches, and, mixed with these, are figures of all kinds—lizards, birds, and pictures of the Buddha. Sometimes women who wish to ensnare the object of their affection endure the pain of having a love charm tattooed upon the tongue or upon the lips. Often a few round spots tattooed with the prescribed formula repeated over it and placed between the eyes will be enough to bring back a wandering lover to her side. If this is not effectual or if the maiden sees herself drifting towards a lonely middle age with no lover in her view, she cuts off the locks of hair hanging over her ears, announcing to all the world that she is looking for a lover. They say in Rangoon that if a woman is tattooed it means that she desires an Englishman for her husband.

In olden days Burmah shared with Japan in the number of its women given in marriage *à la mode* to men of alien races. Nearly every English official and merchant had his house presided over by a little native maiden. These arrangements were very happy, and tragedies did

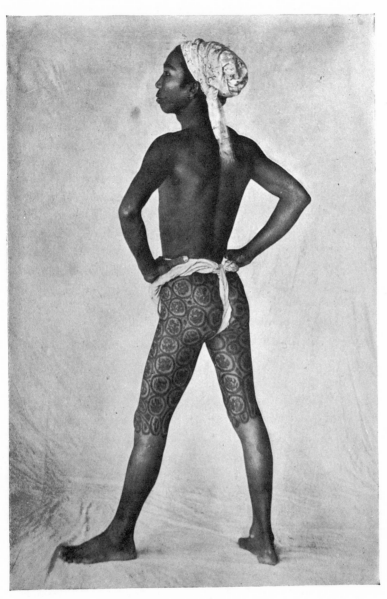

BURMESE BOY WITH TATTOOED LEGS.

To face p. 196.

not occur until the Englishman, longing for home sights and sounds, and the dignity of an English wife, went back home and returned to his station with the woman of his choice. Then there was sorrow, and even the English gold could not repay the little Burmese woman for the loss of the love of the kindly, careless man who had been her master for the many years. Often attempts were made to regain that master's love, and many a time the attempts succeeded, because in the formality and dignity of his English home and the coldness of his English wife, the man remembered the happy days and nights spent under the Burmese roof and the pretty little Burmese girl who shyly slipped her hand in his and called him master, lord of all her days and nights.

There is a story told of an English official in Upper Burmah who, when time for leave of absence came, closed up his Burmese home, giving to its little hostess money sufficient to make her rich for life. On his return to Burmah he brought with him the girl from Devonshire to whom he had been betrothed for many years. At dinner their first night soft steps were heard upon the verandas, and curtains moved as if in the swaying of an evening breeze, but nothing could be seen. The next morning when starting for his office the frightened horse shied madly at a little mound of silk lying by the side of the gateway. It was the little Burmese wife, with a dagger through her heart. Pinned upon her pretty dress was a letter for her lord, in which she said : " I have looked upon thy newly wedded wife and found her good. If I had seen within her eyes—and love would quick have told me—that she were not the worthy one, that she were not fitted to be thy mate through all these years to come, I would have plunged my knife deep in her heart, but now I know it is better for me to go, as life without thee has no joy."

One can understand the charm that these happy, smiling, care-free little women have for the men who come from homes where levity and *laissez-faire* are things to be condemned. The Burmese wife makes no demands upon her lord and master ; she is obedient, attendant to his every want, and never scolding and discontented. As far as material wants are concerned, the native woman of any Eastern country makes an ideal wife for the average European, yet they can never be real companions one with the other. There is more than the bar of language between them ; there is the bar of instincts, customs, and traditions. The entire life of each has been passed in different environments. Practically always the woman has little or no education, and knows nothing of the world outside the town where she was born. There is never any question of equality between the foreign husband and the native wife ; he is always her lord, she is always his slave. To the light-hearted Burmese woman, to whom the marriage tie even with a

EN ROUTE TO A FESTIVAL, BURMAH.

To face p. 198.

man of her own race is not a binding cord,
these "marriages for a day" are not always
things of tragedy, but the curse falls heavily
upon the child if there should be one.   In all
Eastern countries—Egypt, India, Burmah, China,
and Japan—the half-caste is a being set apart.
Ostracized by the members of his father's race,
unrecognized by his mother's people, he is a
social pariah, and one almost feels that, if society
could enforce it, he would be compelled to call
out, "Unclean, unclean!" as did the lepers in
the olden time.

CHAPTER XIII

BURMESE RELIGION AND SUPERSTITION

JUDGING from appearances, the Burmese woman is deeply religious. We see her offering her flowers before the many shrines scattered throughout the country, and hear the deep-toned bell hanging before the lord of light as she strikes it three times to call the attention of the spirits of the air to her piety. On days of festival the pagoda is thronged with gaily dressed women, and at the greatest of all pagoda feasts, that of the Shwe Dagon in Rangoon, women pilgrims from every part of Burmah come to lay their tribute before the greatest shrine in Buddha-land. They come by train and boat and bullock-cart, and to many it is the most important event of the whole year. Girls look forward to the chance it offers to show their charms to the male world, old ladies count on the meeting of friends and the discussion of the events of the past year, while to all it offers a chance to lay up merit for themselves and advance a step on the long road that leads to Neban.

Near the temple are marionette shows, and

theatrical companies make these festivals their place of greatest profit, while the merchants offer their wares for sale, and the sellers of incense, candles, flowers, and offerings for the different shrines reap their harvest. Yet over the whole joyous occasion, which would strike the casual observer as simply a holiday for these happy people, is thrown the veil of a deep religious motive. In the fascination of the secular gaieties around them, these spiritual women do not forget the real object of their pilgrimage, and the prayers and protestations before the altars, and the constant booming of the deep-toned bells, show that praise of the Lord of lords is not forgotten amidst the excitement and pleasures of the world outside.

The Burmese woman may go to the pagoda on the duty days of each month, of which there are four, or she may stay at home. The only force upon her is that of public opinion, yet she generally goes, as it is the meeting-place of all her world, and the care-free Burmese, both men and women, are always looking for a chance of amusement and a meeting with friends.

Whether or not she attends these duty days once a week is solely dependent upon her piety, or her love of companionship; but deeply ingrained within her soul is a daily duty that no Burman, unless of the very advanced class, neglects—the propitiation of the nats, those spirits inhabiting the air, the ground, the water, and all things, both animate and inanimate. Even the stones upon the roadside may be the home of spirits who may prove destructive or hostile at any time. To guard against the evils that might come with neglect of such powerful enemies to his happiness, the Burmese erects a shrine at the extremity of his village, sometimes no larger than a bird house built in the pipul-tree. There he may offer food, and light his tiny lamps, and pour his offerings of water, and burn his incense.

He leaves the nats of the household to the especial care of his wife, who covers all the posts within the rooms with white cloth, so that they may be comfortable while sitting in their favourite places. To counteract the effect of the evil spirits who may wish to take up their dwelling within the home, the careful housewife keeps near at hand a jar of water that has been blessed, and daily sprinkles floor and roof for the protection of her family. It is believed that people who have been executed for their crimes or who have met a violent death become nats and haunt the place where they so suddenly departed from this world, and this belief led to many cruel practices in former times. The burial of men and women alive under the gates of a city originated in this desire to protect its inhabitants, as these spirits wander around the place of their death, and bring disaster upon strangers who may come with evil intent. It is said that under the palace gates fifty men and women were buried alive to protect those within the Imperial residence.

This belief in spirits leads to many evils, and the woman's life is one of constant fear for herself and for her loved ones. She naturally consults in time of trouble with those who have a knowledge of spirit lore, or who have power to control them and make of no avail their wrong intentions. Consequently Burmah abounds in astrologers, necromancers, wizards, and witch-doctors, who impose upon the fears of the women to a marvellous extent. These charlatans vie with the doctors in their ignorance.

A man of medicine in this land ruled by super-stition needs no diploma, and he administers a mixture of herbs and nasty tasting condiments in such strong doses that they are bound to cure or kill. Quantity, not quality, is what the sick Burmese requires ; and if after a medicine is administered five times she is not better, another kind is tried, and if the desired effect is not produced, another doctor is called, who perhaps makes a distinctly different diagnosis of the case, and the dosing is commenced all over again with another set of medicines. It is well known by all that the body is composed of four elements— earth, water, fire, and air—and derangement of these four properties may cause the illness. Before medicine is administered, the horoscope must be consulted in order to learn the proportions of the elements within the body, when perhaps it is found that the sickness is caused by an evil act committed in a former life, or the seasons may be the cause of her misfortune. It is always a most complicated affair, and perhaps the doctor finds that the sufferer must refuse all food whose initial letter begins with the same letter as that of the day of her birth.   There are ninety-six diseases that afflict mankind, and it often takes many doctors and much medicine to decide with which one of the ninety-six ailments the woman is contending.

If she should die, it is believed that the soul, in the shape of a black butterfly, issues from the mouth, and dies at the same time as that of the body which it inhabited.   Although the Buddhists do not believe in the actuality of the soul as we know it, this black butterfly is the real spirit of the woman, and is with her constantly except at times of sleep, when it may leave the earthly body and go roaming over the world.   It can never visit places strange to its owner, as it might lose its way and not come back again, when both would die—the body because its spirit was gone, the butterfly because it had lost its earthly home. One reason why a Burman will not rouse one suddenly from a deep slumber is because he is afraid that the butterfly might be on a visit and unable to return to its home upon the man's awakening, which, of course, would be most fatal. This roaming spirit takes many chances, as there are goblins and evil genii who desire nothing better than to eat black butterflies, and often they become so frightened that they return home in a great panic, which throws the owner of the soul into a fever.   It sometimes happens that the spirit is kept prisoner, and then the witch doctors are brought in and many incantations are gone through to induce the evil gnomes to release their hold upon the poor butterfly before it is too late.

Two souls who deeply love each other often wish to leave the world together, or a mother dies and wishes her loved one, perhaps her only child, to join her in the other land, and her spirit calls for her baby's butterfly, who will follow that of the mother unless frustrated by the machinations of some wise woman who understands the way of spirits. This woman comes to the house, and placing a mirror on the floor by the dead mother or wife who is calling for her child or husband, entreats the dead not to demand the soul of the living. As she pleads with her she allows a piece of down to slip slowly on to the face of the mirror and catches it in a handkerchief, which is then gently placed on the breast of the living, and the spirit comes back to its resting-place.

Superstition dominates the life of the Burmese woman as much as it does her Indian sister. She believes in love potions and philtres to bring a longed-for lover to her side. She consults with wise men, who tell her whether the waning love of husband is caused by the nat or guardian of the house ; or if she is not yet wedded, she finds that the horoscopes of herself and lover are not propitious and that he is not intended for her mate. She also uses this man of science to

revenge herself upon a hated rival, and will cause
an image to be made of clay, over which are
chanted devilish rituals which will cause death or
madness to fall upon the unsuspecting person.

Not only do the spirits of all worlds influence
her, but each act of the things around her has
its meaning. If a hen should lay an egg upon a
cloth, the lucky owner will receive a present ; and
if she is going on a journey and a snake should
cross her path, her misfortune would be certain.
If a dog should carry a bone into the house, she
blesses him, as great riches and honour will come
to all beneath her roof. But she is hampered in
her actions by the number of lucky and unlucky
days that control her destiny. There are days
unfortunate for all the world, and others that
apply only to her, when she must act with exceeding care, and understand the lore of the
stars which were in the ascendant at her birth.
Thursday is generally a good day for all, but if
a woman was so foolhardy as to commence a
work on Tuesday it might be fatal and she would
lose her life. Friday is the day of days on which
to commence a new enterprise, as success is
bound to follow. The hair should be washed
once a month, if possible, but never on Monday,
Friday, or Saturday. A good mother on sending
her son into the monastery would see that the
rite of cutting the hair did not fall upon Monday,
Friday, or his birthday, and it limits the choice
of days, as this latter event, the birthday, occurs
once a week. There are also a few months

A BURMESE WOMAN AND HER CIGAR.

To face p. 206.

especially unlucky for a woman born under certain stars, and no undertaking should be commenced in those months. In fact, the Burmese woman is ruled by signs and omens from her birth to her death, and when the necromancers, the wizards, the doctors, and the witches are unable longer to keep the spirit, the little black butterfly, within the body, and she is gathered to her fathers, rules and traditions govern her laying away to her last resting-place.

In former days the dead were all cremated, but now burying has come into general use. When death comes to a family it means elaborate preparations and feasting from the time that the breath has left the body and the coin is put into the mouth to pay the ferryman for the last journey over the lonely river, until the seven days of mourning are over. Yet it is hard to speak of these days as days of mourning, for music, dancing before the bier, and the feasting in the home would cause the onlooker at a Burmese funeral to believe that he was witnessing a wedding-festival instead of a scene of sorrow.

The Burmese, like most Eastern nations, spend far too much upon their funeral observances; and often a man goes into debt for life to pay for the extravagances which custom and tradition make necessary to uphold his standing in the community when the Angel of Death visits his household.

A new custom, or an old custom made more elaborate, has increased the cost of living for the

hospitable Burman. When invitations are given
for any festivity, the invitation is accompanied
by a present, often a silk handkerchief or a
turban, but with the rich this present is growing
more expensive, until it is becoming a burden
that is causing many of the conservative to
complain. I was told while in Mandalay that
when a certain gentleman sent out invitations
for his daughter's wedding, he accompanied each
invitation with a gold sovereign, and as he bade
more than two hundred guests to the feast, his
entertainment cost him a goodly sum before the
actual expense of the festival took place. This
useless expenditure falls heavily upon the small
official who is trying to live upon his salary, as
salaries are not large in Burmah. A gentleman
with a sense of humour was calling upon us, and
in the course of conversation we touched upon
the servant question. He asked us what a
Chinese butler received for his services in
America. I told him ten pounds a month. He
gasped, and then he laughed and a twinkle came
to his black eyes as he said : " I am an official
of the city of Mandalay, and I receive just that
amount. I think I will go to America."

The Burmese woman in her home is allowed
much more liberty than any other Oriental
woman. She is her husband's equal, although
she is taught to look upon man as a superior
being ; still, that is only theoretical. In actual
life she is one with him in business, his amusements, and in his religious life. He consults

BURMESE WORKING WOMAN.

To face p. 208.

her upon matters of importance, and she has proved worthy of trust and confidence, because she has a good mind and has been allowed to use her judgment in matters of business as well as in her own particular realm—the home. She has domestic troubles with which to contend, but public opinion is helping her, especially in the case of polygamy. This destroyer of woman's happiness is sometimes practised, but sentiment is against it, and it is a very brave man who cares to run counter to the general opinion of his village or city in regard to the number of women he shelters beneath his roof-tree. But if the Burman may not marry more than one woman at a time, he may divorce as many wives as he wishes. As the woman also shares in this prerogative, the law is not so one-sided as it is in Mohammedan countries. Manu, the ancient law-maker, allowed women to divorce their husbands if they were too poor to support them; if they were lazy and would not work; or if they were incapacitated by reason of old age, or became cripples after marriage. The husband may send his wife away if she bears him no male children; if she is not loving; or if she is disobedient. Divorce is purely a personal affair, and the marriage tie may be dissolved at any time the parties concerned think fit, without calling in priest or lawyer.

There are very definite provisions in the laws in regard to the property of the separating couple. In the event of divorce each party takes with

14

them the property brought by them to the new home, and what they accumulated since marriage is either divided by mutual agreement or by a decision of the village elders who sanction the separation.

I am told that divorce is not so common as one would believe, considering the ease with which it may be obtained. The Burman is a very easy-going man, the Burmese wife a clever woman who makes it her business to understand her lord and master, and consequently she generally rules him. " Burmah is the land of henpecked husbands," one Burman told me, " all the world knows our shame "—and then he laughed.

Education is coming more slowly to the Burmese woman than it is to the Indian or the Egyptian. She has not seen its need, consequently has not demanded it. But it will come in time, and the intellectual broadening will free her from the cloud of superstition that now surrounds her and controls her actions to a great extent.

GOLDEN PAGODA, MANDALAY.

To face p. 210.

CHAPTER XIV

THE LADY OF CHINA

IT is not easy for the woman of the Occident to understand the life of the woman of the Orient. The woman of the West, in her freedom, her complex social life, her husband's love, looks pityingly upon the Eastern woman in what appears to be a seemingly restricted sphere—the home. It is known that she is practically a prisoner, not by force but by custom and convention ; that the wall of the compound are the walls of the world to her. It is not realized, however, that there she is supreme, and from within those compound-walls, she sways to a great extent the thought and life of China.

The Chinese lady does not lead a life of leisure or indolence. The picture of the Eastern woman sitting upon divans and eating sweetmeats does not apply to the women of this country. If she is the wife of an official or of a man of wealth, she has a large household over which she must preside. If the husband has a mother living the mother is the head of the house, and her will is absolute. This was shown rather forcibly a few years ago in Peking. The son of a Chinese official while abroad married a European woman. She returned to Peking with her husband, and within a few months fled to a foreign embassy and asked protection, as she believed her life in danger. The mother-in-law had said: " While I was in Europe with you I was power-less, but here I am absolute. I could even kill you and no one would question the act. It is my right to do with you as I wish." The minister could do nothing, as by her marriage the girl had become a Chinese subject and was under the laws of China, which gave the mother of her husband absolute control over her life and person.

Often there are an incredible number of people living under one roof-tree, as all the sons bring their wives to their father's home instead of establishing separate households. Sheng, the director of railways, told me that there were 250 people who took rice each day within his compound. The walls of his garden enclosed a small village. There was a large building con-taining his office and residence. Radiating from this there were rows of smaller houses, where his brothers and married sons lived with their numerous families.

A Chinese house, even of the very rich, is a shabby affair, judged from Western standards. It is always surrounded by a wall, generally painted white. Within the entrance gate is a large wooden screen, placed to insure privacy, and also to guard the doorways from evil spirits, which are known to travel only in straight lines and to abhor corners. If the family is large the home consists of a series of houses built around courtyards. Across the first court are the master's rooms and offices ; then come the houses of the different families, as each wife has a suite of rooms for herself and her children. Some of the wives of the more wealthy Chinese occupy an entire building. The kitchen and the servants' quarters are at the end of the last courtyard.

The floors of all the rooms are of rough boards, with great cracks between them, sometimes covered with a rug but more often bare. The walls are composed of the same wide boards, with here and there an embroidered hanging or a scroll bearing the words of some honoured sage. The furniture of the reception-room consists of small tables alternating with straight-backed chairs, arranged with mathematical precision around the three sides of the room. Opposite the doorway is the seat of honour, or an opium-couch. Often the furniture is elaborately carved or inlaid with mother-of-pearl, but it looks formal and precise. The chairs, with their red embroidered cushions, are very uncomfortable for the Westerner, because of their straight, low backs and high, narrow seats, that make one long for a footstool. There are no buffets nor sideboards in the dining-rooms, and stools are used in place of chairs. The tables are square, seating eight, and neither tablecloths nor napkins are considered necessary adjuncts to dining.

The bedrooms are small, and filled wellnigh to overflowing by an enormous carved bed, with red embroidered curtains hanging from the heavy canopy and long silken tassels draping the four posts. The Chinese do not indulge in mattresses nor springs, sheets, nor pillow-cases. The pillows are small bolsters, and the bedclothing consists of a series of wadded " comfortables " made of silk or cotton. Their dislike of springs is very intense. A hospital for the Chinese was opened in one of the interior towns, and the doctors, wishing to do the very best they could to make their patients comfortable, bought, at great expense, foreign beds with springs. They found, to their disgust, that the patients, as soon as the nurse turned her back, insisted on placing the bedclothing upon the floor and lying there, instead of in the nice comfortable beds that had been provided for them. They claimed that the springs made them " seasick." When Chinese ladies are calling upon a foreign woman, one of the chief ways to amuse them is to take them over the house and permit them to see the furnishings of the homes of the people from over the sea. They are always intensely interested in the beds and look at the springs from all sides, sitting on them and pressing them down with their hands, finally shaking their heads, as much as to say, " It is past all belief what these strange people will have in their houses."

CHINESE WOMEN WARMING HANDS AND FEET WITH BRAZIERS.

To face p. 214.

The chief article of furniture in the kitchen is the stove, a huge affair made of brick. This stove has generally three holes, in which are set the iron cooking-pots, shaped like large wash-bowls and made of very thin metal, in order that the ingredients may cook with the smallest amount of heat necessary, as the question of fuel is a serious one in China. In the country around Shanghai, rice-straw and faggots are the main fuel, while on every hillside in the country one sees women and children cutting the dried grass and gathering every available thing that may be burned. Because of the lack of body in the fuel it keeps one person busy feeding the fire while another attends to the cooking.

The food served at a feast, and which the average foreigner sees, is quite different from that eaten every day. At a feast there are often twenty or thirty courses. Swallow's-nest soup, shark-fins, pigeon eggs cooked with nuts, ducks prepared in many ways, fowl, fish, and innumerable sweets. Rice is served as the last course, while at the ordinary dinner it is the principal dish. It is to the Chinese what bread is to the European or potatoes to the Irish. The food is cooked in vegetable oil, made from beans or cabbages, or, for the richer class, from peanuts. The chief meat is pork, which is cut into little bits and cooked with a vegetable. Beef is not used by the average Chinese. The cow is a beast of burden, and none of her products are eaten. I have seen a great official, on being told that the ice-cream he was eating was made of milk, deposit upon his plate the contents of his mouth with more haste than grace. One receives the impression from pictures that the Chinese politely picks up a few grains of rice with his chopsticks and carries them slowly to his mouth. This is a picture of Occidental imagination rather than Oriental reality. He takes with his chopsticks some vegetables from the dishes in the centre of the table, to which all have access, and, after depositing the chosen morsel on the top of his rice, he lifts the bowl to his face and uses his chopsticks to shovel as much of the rice into the opening as its capacity will permit. The Chinese are supposed to be a slow and phlegmatic race, but if one were to judge by the rapidity with which a bowl of rice will disappear, one would easily give them a place among the most rapid and progressive races of the world.

Food used by the Chinese is very cheap. The Viceroy at Nanking, a man of unlimited wealth and power, told me that the food for himself did not cost more than twenty cents a day. The servants in the American Consulate had their food bought by the second cook, paying him five shillings each per month, which sum included food, cooking, and service. On board a foreign houseboat the captain is paid four shillings per day for the hire of six men, and they are fed by him out of this sum. It is made possible by the cheapness of the vegetables. I have seen him buy three bushels of a curly-

leaved vegetable resembling spinach for two-
pence.

The lady of China takes no part in her husband's business or social life. Much of the
business in China among the official and rich
class is transacted socially, and the dinners are
generally given at a teahouse or restaurant, or
on the pleasure-boats kept for that purpose.
Even the very finest of these entertainment-places
are very shabby affairs, from a Western standpoint. They are also extremely dirty. The
floors are made of unmatched boards that have
never seen the scrubbing-brush, and the guests
throw their fish-bones, cigarette-ends, etc., under
the table.

The Chinese understand the art of dining, and
we who simply go to eat cannot appreciate the
social side of this form of entertainment as does
the Eastern man. He eats a few courses, sheds
a jacket, loosens a belt, talks to a singing girl,
smokes, then eats a few more courses, gambles
a while, and really enjoys himself for four or
five hours. When he enters the room for the
feast he is given a slip of paper, on which
he writes the name of his favourite singing girl
and her place of residence. When all the guests
arrive the slips are taken by a servant to the
different places, and at intervals during the
dinner the girls arrive. These girls are owned
by men or women who bought them when
they were very young, and have trained them
for singing girls or professional amusers. They

sway in on their tiny bound feet, beautifully dressed, painted and powdered, and take their place behind the man who sent for them. They sit on a narrow stool, chat with the man, have a few puffs from a water pipe, eat melon-seeds (they never eat or drink anything from the table) ; then their maid brings them their musical instrument, and they sing, in a high falsetto voice, a song or two. If the song and the singer are admired, the guests show their approval by loud " Hah, hah's." After her song the girl arises, says good-bye to her patron, and leaves for her next engagement. The girl's owner receives from four to sixteen shillings, according to the fame of the girl ; she receives nothing, unless a present is given her by some admirer. Many of them have beautiful bracelets and hair ornaments of pearls and jade, and many own gold water pipes that are very costly. They all carry little make-up boxes, and powder their noses whenever the desire seizes them. To Western eyes they are not pretty, with their red and white faces. They paint their forehead, nose, and around their mouth white, the cheeks and under-lip bright red, and to obtain the proper willow-leaf pattern for the eyebrows their own are shaved and others more slanting are painted in their place. It is hard to see any charm in these little women. They sing through their noses, talk very little, and that the most inane gossip, powder themselves, then bow and go away. They seem to have neither ideas, expression, nor figure.

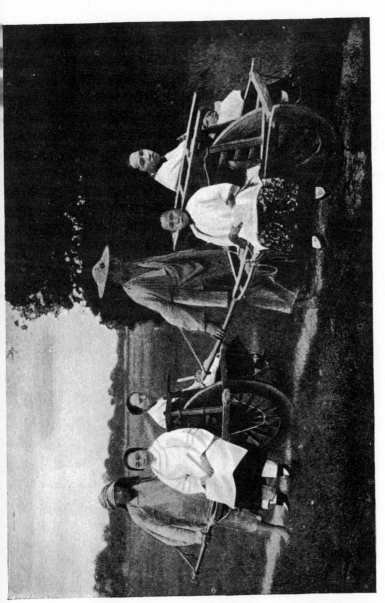

CHINESE WOMEN AND CHAIR-BEARERS.

To face p. 218.

With each one of these entertainers is a maid, who supports her as she sways along on her little feet, and who sees that she does not try to run away from her master. If the girl is popular and in much demand she has a sedan chair and two bearers ; if a very young girl, she is carried on the shoulders of a strong, husky coolie. Many of them lead pitiful lives, and a singing girl's only hope of escape is to become the secondary wife or concubine of a rich man ; then, if she should be so fortunate as to bear a son for her husband she would hold an honourable position, and nothing could be said against her because of her former life.

A Chinese gentleman is out to dinner practically every night, or else he is entertaining friends. He sleeps until noon, goes to his particular club for amusement and to meet his friends in the afternoon, and returns to his home in the wee sma' hours of the night. The wife or wives stay at home and take care of the house and children. No Chinese lady ever dines at a restaurant ; in fact, no Chinese lady ever eats at the same table with her husband ; he would " lose face " if he ate with a woman. Although a lady is never seen dining in public, she frequently gives dinner parties to her friends and relatives. The courtyards are then filled with the chattering chair-bearers, who, squatting on their haunches as only an Eastern servant can, drink innumerable cups of tea served by the servants of the hostess. The guests are met at the entrance to the women's quarters by the lady of the house, and a great many bows are made, varying in depth according to the rank of the guest.

Each guest has a maid, who from time to time brings her mistress a vanity box, from which is extracted powder and rouge ; and she, like her frailer sister, the sing-song girl, applies a little more white to her already whitened nose, or rouges her cheeks, or touches a little red paint to the lower lip. Paint and powder are not confined to the women of the amusement class, as the Chinese lady (that is, the younger ones ; older women do not make up at all) paints her face more than is beautiful to foreign eyes. Even the hands are not forgotten, and within the palms the rouge brush is used. The hands of a Chinese lady are beautiful—long, slender, and delicate, looking as helpless as a flower. In the olden time long fingernails were worn as a mark of ladyhood, and were often covered with jade or gold, telling plainly that the wearer belonged to the leisured class and did not need to toil. In fact, the whole expression of a Chinese lady is helplessness. From her exquisitely coiffured head, with its mass of pearl and jade, to her tiny feet, on which she sways instead of walks, she impresses one as a dainty piece of jewellery, too fragile for real life. The small feet accentuated this, but now they are passing, and the new woman of China is not binding her daughter's feet.

BOUND FEET OF CHINESE WOMAN.

The curse of footbinding does not fall so heavily upon women who may sit and embroider, or if needs must travel can be borne upon the shoulders of their chair-bearers; but it is upon the poor girl, whose parents hope to have one in the family who may better their fortunes by a rich marriage, and, hoping thus, they bind their feet. If this marriage fails and she is forced to work within her household, or, even worse, if poverty compels her to work in the fields, or add her mite gained by most heavy labour to help fill the many eager mouths at home, then she should have our pity. We have seen the small-footed woman pulling heavy boats along the tow-paths, or leaning on their hoes to rest their tired feet while working in the fields of cotton. To her each day is a day of pain, and this new law forbidding the binding of the feet of children will come as a blessing from the gods. But it will not pass at once, as so many now loudly proclaim; it will take at least three generations: the children of the present children will quite likely all have natural feet. The people in the country, far from the noise of change and progress, will not feel immediately that they can wander so far afield from the old ideas of what is beautiful in their womenkind.

The most noticeable thing about a Chinese woman, poor as well as rich, is her hair: it is jet-black, and made shiny and smooth with a paste until not a strand is out of place. At certain times of the year small wreaths are made from tiny yellow flowers and placed around the knot at the back. The hair is never untidy, and the artistic disorder of the hair of the foreign woman is secretly much disliked by the Chinese. The late Empress-Dowager once gave the wife of a foreign Minister a set of combs as a present. The Minister's wife was delighted, as the gift was enclosed in an elaborate silver box, and she did not see the subtle suggestion in the present, over which the Chinese of the province chuckled for many a day.

A party of Chinese ladies presents a very gay appearance. They wear silk or satin, nearly always brocaded and often heavily embroidered. In the winter, as the houses are not heated, many furs are worn, but almost entirely, except in the case of sable, as linings for the silken coats. One garment is put on over the other until the right degree of warmth is obtained. Instead of speaking of degrees of cold, the Chinese say it is three-coat weather or five-coat weather. The children are clothed in wadded garments, so thick that the overdressed babies look like little round balls and can scarcely move. In the summer the ladies wear delicate gauzes over their under-garments of grass-linen.

Nearly every province in China has its own customs and peculiarities in dress as well as in everything else, but they all agree on the rich reds and blues, the purples and mauves for the making of their jackets, while their wide, skirt-like trousers are often of a much deeper colour than the jacket and trimmed with a wide band of black. The mixture of tints sounds most incongruous to foreign ears, but Chinese women have the faculty of weaving the most clashing hues into a work of harmonious art. Except in the case of an old lady, black is seldom worn, and as white is the colour of mourning, it is seen only on occasions of sorrow. A Chinese lady can never understand why European babies are dressed in white. Children are the symbols of happiness, and it seems to them most inappropriate to garb them in sorrow's colours. All the gayests and brightest colours of China's dye-pots are made to produce the clothing for China's children.

The dress of the Chinese woman, rich or poor, is very modest, fastening close around the neck, with sleeves coming to the hands and the loose jacket formed so as to disguise the lines of the body. European women are severely censured in China because of their *décoleté* gowns and tight dresses, which seem to the Chinese the height of vulgarity. When one of the Imperial princes was *en route* to England, he attended his first foreign dinner in Shanghai. About twenty-five of the guests were English and American ladies, dressed in their most elaborate gowns, which means extreme *décolleté*. The attachés of the prince had tried to prepare his highness for the sight he was to witness ; but they had evidently underestimated its startling qualities, because when the prince arrived and

gave one amazed look at his hostess and the line
of waiting ladies he was nonplussed. He looked
pitifully for his interpreter, and, not receiving
aid from him, put down his head, shut his eyes,
and bravely stumbled around the room, groping
blindly for each lady's hand, as he had been
informed that he should shake hands with them.
This was another serious breach of Chinese
etiquette, as no Chinese man must ever touch
a woman. The Chinese views in regard to
modesty connected with the dress of women has
caused the missionaries in the interior to expur-
gate from the magazines that may by chance fall
into the hands of Chinese visitors all pictures
of lightly clad ladies who are used to advertise
soaps and powders and the underwear of our
American markets.

The Chinese are very fond of their children.
They say, " In the children our parents return
to us ; in the children we live again."   When
ladies visit each other they always ask for the
children, who are brought in by the nurses. With
their jackets of red, their trousers of bright green
or purple, their baby-caps with its rows of tiny
brass Buddhas that shine and glitter like gold,
and the mark of red paint on the forehead or on
the tip of the tiny nose, they look like brilliant
little elfs. The girls are dressed quite as richly
as the boys, and it is to the interest of the nurse
to make the children as attractive as possible,
because the pleased visitor generally gives her
a small present of money wrapped in red paper.

AN OLD-FASHIONED CHINESE GIRLS' SCHOOL.

To face p. 224.

Visiting a high-class Chinese lady, one is impressed with the number of children and servants that seem to be swarming over the place. When one of a family has distinction or wealth, all the poor relatives come to dwell with him. Li Hung-chang built a home in Shanghai in which to live when he should retire from private life. When asked why he built so far from his home province, which was contrary to Chinese custom, he said he built as far as possible from his native town, hoping that his poor relations could not obtain the money with which to come to Shanghai.

The servants in a Chinese family are not expensive, so far as wages are concerned, but they cost a great deal in perquisites. They rarely receive more than eight shillings a month, but they are given their food, and they help themselves lavishly to anything they may desire. They dress themselves from the old clothing of the family, freely take the hairpins and the toilet articles of the mistress, clothe their children from the common wardrobe, and, in fact, are a part of the family.

There is a peculiar democratic custom which servants may claim, but which is seldom used— the right of reviling the family when discharged. The youngest son of Li Hung-chang lived next door to me, and an old serving-woman was discharged for a reason that evidently did not appeal to her sense of justice. She sat beneath the gateway and for three hours called down curses

15

upon the Li family at the top of her voice. This happened on one of the principal residence streets of Shanghai, and the police passed and repassed, but no one tried to stop her. The house steward made two or three feeble attempts to persuade her to leave, but she would turn her facile tongue upon him, and he would gather his skirts in his hands and start on a most undignified run for the house, evidently believing discretion to be the better part of valour. At the end of three hours, when she was completely exhausted, she was led away.

The Chinese lady and her servants gossip together as friends, rooms are entered without warning, conversations interrupted, and suggestions offered which, to the foreigner, seem to be of the grossest impertinence. This intimacy is due partly to the restricted life the lady leads, and partly to the fact that many of the servants are distant relatives. Practically the only news from the outside world that comes to the woman behind the walls is brought by her sons or by the servants. She makes few visits, and these usually at the home of some relative, entering her closely covered chair within her courtyard and carried swiftly to the courtyard of the house where she is to visit. There is no such thing as " calling " between the wives of men who are mutually interested in affairs or who are business associates. The wife of a Treaty Commissioner called upon the wives of the Chinese officials who were associated with her husband in conducting the treaty. They were very polite and returned her call, but are still wondering *why* she called.

The wife of a consul wished to give a luncheon to the wife of the Mayor of Shanghai. She asked the interpreter who was assisting her in the arrangements if other Chinese ladies of the same rank might be asked. The interpreter said, " No ; a Chinese lady would rather not meet women other than relatives."

The Chinese wife lives entirely for her family and with her family. She rarely goes to a public place of amusement, although in some of the ports, like Shanghai and Canton, entire families are seen at the Chinese theatres. Theatrical companies come to the houses of the rich and official class for the amusement of guests, and story-tellers and musicians, nearly always blind, go from door to door asking to be taken into the women's courtyards to help while away the dreary hours. Astrologers and fortune-tellers pass along the resident streets, striking their little gong to attract the notice of the women behind the walls. They are extremely clever, and cast horoscopes in a manner similar to that of the Egyptians of olden times. They are very popular among the Chinese women, as are fortune-tellers with women of all races.

We are prone to sympathize with the Chinese woman because of the plurality of wives, but one sees little evidence of the need of our sympathy. The Chinese have a saying : " The head wife should cherish the inferior wives as the great tree cherishes the creepers that gather round it." I do not know whether this sage advice is always followed, but I have seen the several wives of many officials, all friendly as sisters and all working for the common good of the home.

I called upon the wife of an official and was met at the door by two ladies. One of them was a very old Chinese lady, with the smallest bound feet that I have ever seen ; they could not have been more than $2\frac{1}{2}$ inches in length. She was partially supported on one side by a servant, and on the other by a beautifully dressed Manchu woman. After I was seated in the place of honour at the left of the elderly lady, and tea was brought, I asked the usual question, " What is your honourable age? " She replied, " Sixty-two " ; then, as always follows, I said, " How many children have you? " She replied, " Five." I asked their ages, and, to my astonishment, heard her say that the eldest was seventeen years and the youngest two months. When I could find words to continue the conversation, I turned to the Manchu lady and asked her practically the same questions. She replied that she was thirty-five years old, was the mother of five children, the eldest being seventeen years and the youngest two months. Then I realized that the first wife had no children, but, according to Chinese custom, claimed as her own all children born to the secondary wives.

The custom was further exemplified by the wife of a magistrate who was calling upon me, accompanied by the second wife. After the usual questions in regard to age and health, I asked this lady how many children she possessed. She looked at me in a puzzled manner for a moment, then turned to the other wife and, keeping track of the names by turning down a finger at each count, said: " Let me see— how many children have I? Tsai-an has three, Wo-kee has five—that is eight; Ma-lu has two— ten; Sin Yun has four—fourteen; Sih-peh two —sixteen; and you have three "; then, turning to me, she said, " I have nineteen children."

I have a Chinese friend who lived in Canton until he became involved in some political trouble that caused him to leave for Shanghai, where he would be under the protection of the foreign settlements. He left behind him his mother, four wives, and sixteen children. He became lonely in his exile, and asked his mother to send him a couple of his wives. She wrote him that they were busy attending to the education of their children, and that they did not speak the dialect in Shanghai and would feel like strangers; consequently it would be better for him to marry a couple of women native to the province, who would be more contented. He took her advice.

There is an American woman doctor in Shanghai who goes to the homes of the rich Chinese in the practice of her profession. I

asked her one day if she knew the wife of
Mr. Lu, a prominent merchant who had a most
beautiful home on the smart drive in Shanghai.
She replied that she knew a part of her—numbers
one, four, seven, and eleven. A rich man is
only restricted in the number of wives he may
possess by his ability to support them. Gossip
says—I do not know how true it is—that Yuan
Shi-kai has the unlucky number of thirteen wives
beneath the roof-tree of the President's palace
in Peking.

One would naturally suppose that endless complications of a disagreeable nature, leading to
quarrels and bitterness, would arise, yet there
does not seem to be more unhappiness in the
average Chinese home than in those of any other
country. The first wife, she who has been chosen
by the parents, is the head of the household, and
her word is law, the other wives practically occupying the position of servants. That is the
theory, but in actual practice she who is fortunate enough to be the mother of sons, or
perhaps the last girl-wife, is generally the
favourite, and wields great influence over the
master of the household. I said to a woman
calling upon me one day that I should not feel
so badly after the first wife was chosen to replace
me, but that the choice of my immediate
successor would make me very unhappy. She
looked astonished, and said : " That depends
entirely upon the woman. If she is agreeable
and pleasant, it is a pleasure to have her

in the family.   Often a first wife chooses a second."

We of the Western world look upon a great many wives as a luxury only to be enjoyed by the very rich.   I have a friend who is very intimate in a Chinese family in which there are five wives. Since hearing her talk I have changed my mind in regard to the luxury of the plurality of wives. In this household the first wife lives with the husband's family at their country place ;   the other four live with him.   The husband supplies a cook for the common use of the family, and this cook provides rice, the staple article of food for the household.   Each wife is given a servant and one pound a month with which to buy her luxuries, and once a year she is given a complete suit of silk or satin clothing, and if a favourite, I presume she receives jewels, etc., from her husband.   A man told me that in the interior of China (Shanghai, Peking, and some of the larger cities are much more expensive) he could support easily his four wives and fourteen children on an income of £200 a year.

There are many foolish women who marry attachés of the Chinese embassies in England and America, or, more foolish still, who marry a Chinese merchant.   They are, in fact, marrying the romance of the East represented to them in the person of the suave little almond-eyed man, and they pay bitterly for their mistake if they ever return to their husband's country.   They are recognized by neither Chinese nor foreigners, have no social standing in any community, and lead an existence that calls for pity.

There lived in Shanghai a man who had once been a secretary of the Legation in London. He had a great career ahead of him until he married an Englishwoman, when he was ordered home, degraded, and lived for years as the petty official in the office of the mayor of the city, at a wage scarcely liveable even for a Chinese. His wife, recognized by neither English nor Chinese, became addicted to opium and drink, and died after a few years of unhappiness. A woman doctor told me that she found the body lying in an outhouse, on a bundle of straw, waiting for burial, where finally it found a resting-place in a Chinese cemetery.

A few years ago a woman came to the English Consul in Nanking and asked for protection. She had married a Chinese merchant in London, and on his return to his own country he met with business reverses that reduced him practically to the position of a coolie. She had been forced to go into the paddy-fields transplanting rice. It is bad enough to see a Chinese woman standing in the mud and water to her knees, doing this back-breaking work, but it would be heartrending to see a woman of our race toiling alongside of the ignorant Chinese peasant, under the rays of the tropical sun, which beats down so pitilessly upon the exposed rice-fields. The Consul was extremely sorry for the woman, but could not interfere in the domestic life of a

Chinese subject. When she found nothing could be done for her, she took the little round ball of sleep with which so many Chinese wives pass across the bridge of death—opium.

If these women who think that it would be such a wonderful experience to live in the glorious East, of which they have read most glittering tales, would realize that when the man returns to his homeland his parents have the right of choosing a wife for him, who is his real wife, and the poor foreign woman is reduced to the position of a concubine, I think many of them would not take a step so fatal to happiness. Dr. Barchet, of the Baptist Mission near Ningpo, saw an American woman living in a small village who was one of four wives, all occupying the same peasant's cottage. When asked why she did not return to her homeland, she said that she was ashamed to have her people learn of her great mistake, as she married against their wishes. The bad air and coarse food were having their effect upon this delicately raised girl, and she was a victim to the great white plague that claims so many lives in China.

Suicide is very common among the women of China. When the mother-in-law becomes too oppressive, or life becomes intolerable from other causes, the wife often takes the law into her own hands and takes opium or jumps into the well. She then not only receives surcease from her sorrows, but, according to Chinese superstition, her spirit will linger around the home, haunting and tormenting the person who was the cause of her taking the fatal step.

There is very little intercourse between foreign and Chinese women. The latter do not seem to care about making the acquaintance of the women from over the seas. It is only of late years that the wives of foreign officials in Shanghai have had any intercourse with the families of the local officials. Such intercourse consists simply in an interchange of calls, and a luncheon given once a year by the wife of the senior Consul, and returned by the wife of the Chinese taotai or mayor. There can never be any degree of friendship between the Chinese woman and the European. Their lives are radically different ; the Chinese woman's ideals are not the same as those of her foreign sister. Their only common subject of conversation is in regard to their children ; and even there a bar is soon put across the conversation, as the Chinese mother has different hopes and ambitions for the future of her children than those of the woman from England or America. She knows nothing of the outside world, and her only subjects of conversation relate to household gossip, clothes, and the actions of her friends. In Shanghai a society is formed that is trying to bring the women of all nationalities into touch with one another, but it is not a very great success so far as the Chinese lady is concerned. She feels awkward and ill at ease in the presence of these women, who talk so easily on matters of which she knows nothing, and she much prefers the quiet of her courtyards, amidst the life she understands.

When a Chinese lady is persuaded to go into the world she is always most dignified, even under embarrassing circumstances. I once gave a luncheon for the wife of a Governor of a province, to which the wives of the consuls and a few other ladies were invited, about twenty in all. When the guest of honour arrived all the other guests rose to meet her. As she entered the doorway her tiny bound feet stepped upon a rug, which slipped from beneath her, and instead of swaying gently across the room she sat down and slid to the feet of her astonished hostess. She was helped to rise by the frightened guests, and turned and shook hands with them gravely, without a flicker of the eyelids to indicate that sliding was not the usual mode of entering a drawing-room.

The Chinese lady is trained not to show emotion of any kind. Her face, to be beautiful, must be absolutely placid, care-free, " like unto the full moon in its glory." They consider the foreign woman extremely ugly, with their long, care-lined faces. They say that if it were not for the clothing they could not distinguish men from women. Their faces, with their prominent noses and deep-set eyes, appear to them coarse and unrefined. I have seen children when suddenly confronted with a foreign woman scream in terror.

The Chinese do not impress the casual visitor as a nervous people. It is said that they can bear without murmuring the most severe punishments, and a torture that would reduce a foreign man to frenzy will elicit only a groan from a member of this phlegmatic race. The women seem to share with their menfolk in this lack of " nerves." I once made a visit to the wife of the city magistrate, whose home was in the official " yamen." She showed me over her house, and on entering her bedroom I went to the only window in the room to see what kind of a view was to be obtained. What was my horror to find that the window looked directly upon the punishment courtyard, where a man was then being held down upon his face and a bamboo vigorously applied by the lictor. The moans of the victim could be faintly heard, and what it would be in the summer-time, when the windows were open, could very well be imagined. I turned to my hostess and said, " How frightful ! How can you stand it ? " She shrugged her shoulders and said, " Oh, one becomes used to it."

The Chinese woman is very devout, and observes all the feast-days and days of fasting. It is really the woman who keeps up the religion of Confucius and Buddha. An official who had just returned from sacrificing to the dragon who was supposed to have swallowed the sun at the time of an eclipse, was asked if he believed in this dragon. He laughed and said, " Of course

WHEELBARROW AND COOLIE—USED IN PLACE OF WAGONS IN TOWNS AND COUNTRY VILLAGES NEAR SHANGHAI.

To face p. 236.

not." " Then," the curious questioner continued,
" why do you do it? " He said, " Why do men
in America go to church? Mainly because their
wives wish them to go. It is the same here.
It is the women who are the spiritual force of
China. It is they who are devout, and it is they
who keep open the temples and preserve the
belief in the gods."

The Chinese woman's religion is difficult of
definition, but whatever she is, a follower of the
teachings of Confucius or of the Great Buddha,
she turns to her gods both in time of trouble
and in time of thanksgiving. It is a real factor
in her life. Buddhism has a great festival in
the spring, about the time of our Easter. Then
the roads are covered with processions of women
going or coming from the temples. All ranks
are seen—the lady borne swiftly along in her
sedan-chair with the spirit money hanging from
the poles ; the middle-class woman riding on
the passenger wheelbarrows with four or five
of her friends, with her incense and candles in
her lap ; and the poor woman trudging along the
stone-covered road, carrying her offerings in a
basket of rice-straw which she has woven at
home. When they arrive at the temple they
are all of one great sisterhood. The spirit money
of rich and poor alike is placed in the great
incense-burner in the outer courtyard, where it
goes up in flames to the gods. Then the temple
is entered, the candles are lighted, and the
incense is placed before the particular deity

whose kind offices they implore ; the head is touched to the floor, prayers are uttered, and the woman returns to the courtyards, where she may pass the time with her friends, feeding the carp in the ponds or admiring the great trees which are found within the courts of many of the big temples. If a special boon is to be asked, or if there is doubt and trouble, she takes a hollow bamboo vase, about the size of a quart measure, in which are a couple of dozen sticks of slit bamboo. She kneels three times, touching her head to the floor each time, then shakes the bamboo with a rotary motion until one of the sticks detaches itself from the others and falls to the floor. This she takes to a priest, who reads the number upon it and gives her a slip of yellow paper covered with Chinese characters, and from it she will find the answer to her prayers. It takes considerable imagination to obtain solace from one of these pieces of paper, as they are made to fit all cases, and carry about as much meaning as does the " fortune " on the card handed one by the figure in the slot-machine for which we pay a penny.

The gods are not only worshipped at the temples, but religious adoration plays an important part in the home-life. Over the kitchen stove, in a niche, reposes the household god. From that high place he watches all that goes on within the household. He knows the sins of commission and the sins of omission. Once a year he is taken down and with great ceremony burned and sent up to the Great God to report upon the actions of the household for the year, and a new god is installed in his place. In the meantime he is propitiated in various ways. The first thing in the morning a small bowl of rice and another of water is placed before him, and incense and candles are burned daily at his feet to gain his favour.

Priests are frequent visitors at the homes, and religious ceremonies attend all the great family events, like the first shaving of the baby's head, or that most important day when the mother attains her fiftieth year. This is a day of general rejoicing, when her children unite and buy the happy mother the greatest and most precious present she can receive—her grave-clothes. They are presented amidst much feasting, and chanting of prayers, and burning of candles and incense, and the mother is congratulated by all her friends for the blessing of such filial children.

CHAPTER XV

THE RED CHAIR OF MARRIAGE

THE home must have its basis in marriage, and to that important episode in woman's life the greatest attention is given. In China, as in India, the betrothal ceremony is as binding as the marriage, although I am told that the "new woman" of China is rebelling at the child betrothals and the lack of freedom granted her in the choice of a mate. It is said that in Shanghai a couple who have been betrothed in childhood by their parents, on arriving at marriageable age, may go before a magistrate and repudiate the agreement, and in many instances their cases have been upheld even against the protests of father and mother. This shows the most extreme progressiveness of present-day China, as hitherto a child, especially a girl, was simply a chattel to be disposed of according to the dictates of the nearest male relative. Still, with the exception of the foreign settlement of Shanghai, the old customs of betrothal and marriage prevail, and the principals in the marriage have very little to say in regard to the disposal of their future.

240

Often children are betrothed before their birth by parents, who, being good friends and desiring to unite the families, agree that if a boy is born in one family and a girl in the other, they shall marry. Other matches are made by a professional " go-between," who is employed by the parents of either the boy or girl to find a suitable alliance for their child. This " go-between " is so thoroughly recognized that the Chinese have a saying, " Without a go-between no happy marriage can be effected."

After the search culminates in the discovery of the bride and groom of equal social standing and endowed with the proper amount of this world's goods, the names of the girl and boy are written upon a paper and taken to the necromancer, who decides whether the marriage will be fortunate. Every child is born under the protection of some animal ; if the protecting animal of the daughter is a sheep and that of her fiancé a lion, naturally they should not marry. But if the guardian animal of the bride-to-be should be a bird, they will live in peace with one another. The girl must be thirteen or fifteen or seventeen years of age, as an even number would be most unlucky. Seventeen years is about the average marriageable age of a Chinese girl at present, although formerly they married when hardly more than children.

The marriage customs are essentially the same all over China. The husband gives a certain sum of money to the bride's parents, which varies with the position of the families. Among the poor the girl is practically sold, although the money is supposedly used for the purchase of the wedding outfit. The bride's standing in the family of the husband often depends largely upon the trousseau and the furnishings she takes with her to her new home.

The outfit a girl of the middle class should take with her, in order that she might command the proper respect of her new relatives, should include three red trunks, one table, two chairs, one wardrobe, three tubs, two buckets, one wash-stand, one dressing-case, a set of scissors, a foot-stove, a teapot, wine-pot, two candlesticks, a basin, sugar-bowl, tea-caddy, one set of cups, a complete set of bowls and dishes, two wadded quilts, two embroidered pillows, embroidered curtain for the bed, and a complete outfit of clothing.

This donation of the bride's parents to the formation of a new home is carried before the bride in the wedding procession. Often musicians herald the coming of a bride, who, from her closely covered red chair, watches with beating heart the procession taking her to her new mother-in-law, who can make of her future home a prison or a palace of love. When she finally arrives at the house, that is decorated with red hangings and long scrolls of red silk and flowers, both real and artificial, she sees her husband for the first time as she steps over the threshold. After the one quick look, they go before the ancestral tablet, and, kneeling, touch their heads three times to the floor. Thus she shows that she is now one of the family, worshipping her husband's ancestors instead of those of her own family ; and after prostrating themselves before her husband's parents and drinking from the same cup as a symbol of their unity, they retire to a room, where they sit upon two red chairs and the merry-making begins. Their friends come in, and, facing them, try to make the bride laugh, showing that she will be a most frivolous woman. There is much music, feasting, and playing of tricks on this joyous occasion, and for this little woman, dressed in red satin embroidered in gold, with a big crown upon her head and bead-fringe hanging over her face, the three days of the wedding festivities are most wearying. But she realizes that she must enjoy them if she can, because after they have passed she settles down into the daughter-in-law, which too often proves to be almost the place of a slave, or at the most a household drudge. One can imagine the discord and strife there is within a household where there are several sons who are married, each bringing his wife to his parents' home. I knew a family of grandparents, parents, and children numbering thirty-eight, all living in one modest house. We can understand the Chinese savant making the character for discord a roof with two women under it.

Often in a rich girl's dowry are slave-girls, and although it is really against the law to own slaves, it is, in fact, one of the great evils of China. These helpless people are owned by even the poor. The mother of my maid possessed two slave-girls whom she had bought when very young. She treated them well, and when they grew to marriageable age expected to find husbands for them, giving them an outfit of clothing and a small dowry. In times of famine girls are sold for very small amounts of money or exchanged for the more precious rice. This seems most cruel ; but in order that the rest of the family may live, one must be sacrificed. When everything of value is sold, when the winter clothing is in the pawnshop, when there is no rice to give to crying children, then there is but one thing left for the despairing mother, she must sell her daughter. Chinese mothers are the same as mothers from all over the world, and she only parts with her little girl as a last resort, to the merchants who follow the disasters and fatten on the misery of the Chinese peasant. When it has become known that a famine has made desperate the poor of a province, the merchants from the tea-houses and the brothels of the great cities go to the little towns and villages in the track of the famine, and buy the girls from the fathers and mothers, who can see nothing but death ahead for all unless they sacrifice one. The clever, pretty girls are trained for the tea-houses, inmates of brothels, or concubines of rich men. The ugly, stupid ones are domestics, and often are most cruelly treated.

The owners prefer buying the girl very young, from five to seven years of age, when she can be more easily trained. If she is a pretty girl, her feet must be bound, and if this is a cruel operation under the tender hands of a mother, how much more dreadful it may become when attended to by some one whose only thought is to profit by the girl's beauty!

The slaves in a rich family fare very well. Each child is given one or two personal servants, and when the children grow up and marry they follow them to the new home. Often a pretty, attractive slave-girl becomes the secondary wife of her master, and if she should be so fortunate as to bear him sons, she ranks with her mistress in the honour given her within the household.

There is a home in Shanghai for the rescue of little girls whose mistresses are more than ordinarily cruel. There is also a branch of the Florence Crittenden work for the rescue of girls sold to tea-houses. It is very hard for the people who are engaged in this good work to obtain the girls unless they are so badly treated that it comes to the notice of the magistrate, who may send the girl to the home for a given period.

I saw a pitiful case at a hospital at Soochow. We were sitting in the clinic when a very pretty woman came in and threw herself on her knees before the doctor and began to cry. She said between her sobs: " Oh, foreign doctor, help me to get away, help me, help me!" She was a respectable girl from Ningpo who had been sold by her husband to a place in Soochow for four years. She loathed the life, and when for the first time she had eluded the old woman who always goes out with these unfortunates to see that they do not get away, she had appealed to the only hope she knew. Yet that appeal was useless, as nothing could be done for her. She was nothing but a chattel of her husband, according to Chinese law, and he had a perfect right to sell her if he wished. I saw another pretty girl of sixteen who had been sold for eighty dollars to the same place. She came to the hospital to have her back treated, as she had been severely beaten with a brick because she would not make herself sufficiently pleasing to a guest.

But the average Chinese girl goes to her husband's home quite likely within a short distance of her girlhood village, and passes a most uneventful life, one day being exactly like another unless broken by the ceremonies attending the births, weddings, and deaths of her husband's people. Every village is surrounded by trees and is exactly like its neighbour, with its one-story, thatched-roof houses, or, perhaps, if the owner is especially prosperous, the pointed roofs may be formed of blue-grey tiling. Part of the front yard is beaten and made smooth to be used for threshing the rice, the front room of the house is used for the storing of the farming implements, and the other rooms are given to the different members of the family according to their needs. There is no light and little venti-

RAIN-COATS OF CHINESE WORKMEN.

To face p. 246.

lation in these rude village homes. Windows are expensive and cold, as the houses are not heated in the winter. The mothers may be seen sitting in their doorways, holding in their hands brass hand-warmers, in which are a few burning coals of charcoal, and under their feet are the braziers which provide the only heat for these poor people during the cold months of the year.

The life lived by these village people is life reduced to its simplest form. The main food is rice and a little cabbage. Meat is an unknown quantity unless on special feast days. Beef is not used, as the cow is a beast of burden, and the Chinese have the same feeling in regard to its flesh that we have for the flesh of horses. Ducks, chicken, eggs, fish, crabs, snails, and clams are the poor man's luxuries. No hole is too muddy nor water too filthy for a fish-net to be drawn across it, or for the little crowd of boys who catch the crabs to help fill the family pot.

The question of clothes is a simple one and easily solved. The father wears a pair of blue cotton trousers in the summer, while the mother wears the same style garment with the addition of an apron effect which covers the bust. An amulet and a string are sufficient clothing for the children during the warm days, but when winter comes the wadded clothing must be brought forth, often from the pawnshop, where it goes in the spring to obtain money to buy the seed for planting.

The great prayer which rises from the heart

of all Chinese women, rich and poor, peasant and princess, is to Kwan-yin for the inestimable blessing of sons. " Sons, give me sons ! " is heard in every temple. A woman is not honoured until she has sons to worship at the tablets of her husband's ancestors. One of the chief reasons for divorce in China is the lack of sons, and if the first wife has no male children, and the secondary wife has borne sons to her lord, the lot of the first wife is very bitter. In one of the foreign hospitals in Shanghai for Chinese women, the wife of an official in Tientsin gave birth, much to her sorrow, to a girl. She was inconsolable, and would not allow the dreadful news to be sent to her home, and the doctors feared that she would take her life. But through a servant the unhappy woman saw a way to regain the love and respect of her family. At the same time that the daughter was born to her a beggar-woman in the charity department gave birth to a boy. She bought the boy and telegraphed her husband, " Thou art the father of twins."

One of the upper servants in a consulate, growing rich on the foreign spoils, took to himself a second wife, giving as his excuse that he had four daughters and no sons. At the birth of a son to the new wife the first wife tried to starve herself to death, and failing that, took opium and gained her wish. She could not survive the ignominy of being only the mother of girls.

Sons mean so much to a Chinese mother that she feels that the gods must be jealous of her happiness, consequently she puts an ear-ring in one ear of her boy to deceive the god and make him think the loved one is a girl. She also calls him her " ugly one," her " stupid one," or simply gives him a number so the gods will not see how much he is loved and covet her treasure. There is an economic reason behind all this love for the man-child. A poor Chinese, a workman, cannot save enough money to provide for even his simple wants in his old age. Try as he may, he can only earn enough to live upon from day to day, but if he has sons he knows that when old age comes, and he can no longer work, that care will be given him and he will not want. There is no crime so great as the lack of filial piety, and the State punishes severely the son who does not provide for his aged parents. Indeed, of the five punishments of the criminal code directed against three thousand offences, disobedience or neglect of parents is the most severe.

An illustration of this occurred not long ago in the interior of China. A man arose in the night at the sound of a burglar, and in the struggle in the dark the robber was killed. On bringing a light it was found that the robber was the father of the man whose house he entered. He was known to be a ne'er-do-well, but the unparalleled act of killing one's own father aroused intense excitement in the whole province. The case was deemed of such importance that it could not be tried by the local magistrate, but it was transferred to the courts in Peking, which condemned the man to death, not because he killed the robber, but because his father had evidently been compelled to rob for a living.

Another similar case came to the notice of the foreigners in Shanghai. A man accidentally hit his father with a hoe, causing his death. The whole village took the man to the city, but while on the road they met the magistrate, who asked them not to bring the dreadful case before him officially, but for the clan or village to mete out the punishment and then report to him. They buried the son alive.

Missionaries from a town in the interior asked the American Consul to intervene in the case of a boy nine years old, who, while in play, allowed a stool accidentally to slip from his hand, hitting his mother on the head and killing her. He was condemned to death, but because of his youth was to be kept in prison until he was sixteen, when he would pay the penalty. The Consul did all in his power to save the boy, but, outside of friendly arguments, nothing could be done, as he was a Chinese subject and came under the jurisdiction of Chinese courts of law.

Because of this necessity for the provision for the old age of parents, there are no homes for the aged nor houses for the poor in China, unless one excepts those established through foreign influence. Each family must take care of its own helpless, and if a person is so unfortunate as to have no family, the begging bowl by the roadside is the only recourse when the years are many and the once strong arms are weak.

The filial piety and respect for parents that are so strongly entrenched in the Chinese character causes the son to obey his father until the day of his death. I know a man fifty years of age who was offered the post of secretary of the Embassy in London, but who declined this very advantageous position because his mother did not want him to go to a foreign land. He gave up willingly the chance of a lifetime rather than cause sorrow to his mother in her old age.

A mission in a certain town was very desirous of buying a certain piece of ground on which to erect a church, and the plan was balked by the local official. The missionary conducting the negotiations could find no suitable reason for the official's action in the matter, and finally asked the help of his consul. The taotai was firm in his refusal, and offered the mission land in another part of the city for their church. When pressed for a reason for his refusal he finally said : " My mother passes that place each time she goes to her favourite temple, and she objects to a building holding a foreign god being erected there. She thinks it would pollute the good spirits of the air. I know it is what you call superstition, but she is my mother and I must obey her wishes."

Family life has been from time immemorial the foundation-stone of the Chinese Empire, and filial piety is the foundation-stone of the family

life. The Chinese is taught that the interest of
the family is always of greater importance than
the interest of the individual. This respect and
veneration is not only for the living, but also
for the dead. The death days of two generations of parents are kept sacred with solemn
rites, and every home has its family shrine, to
which all the members must pay due reverence.

This respect and worship is paid by the woman
to the ancestors of her husband's family, as it is
her destiny on reaching womanhood to go to a
new home and live in submission to her new
parents, and burn incense before the shrines of
her husband's people. When she marries she
practically leaves her home for ever. If she is
returned to it—that is, if she is divorced—" shame
shall cover her to her latest hour." Divorce is
very rare in China, but there are seven reasons
given for divorcing a wife. The first is disobedience to father- or mother-in-law, barren-
ness, lewdness, leprosy, over-much talking, and
stealing.

The woman is taught that her lifelong duty
is obedience. Her husband must be looked upon
as " heaven itself," and she must pay all outward
respect to his parents. Her first duty each morning is to bring a cup of tea to the bedside of her
husband's mother, and to bow her head before
her as a sign of submission and respect. She
is taught that the only qualities that benefit a
woman are gentle obedience, chastity, quietness,
and mercy, and that the five worst infirmities

that may afflict a female are indocility, discontent, slander, jealousy, and silliness. Confucius says : " These five vices are found in seven or eight out of every ten women, and it is from these that arise the inferiority of the sex."

Generations of this teaching has made the Chinese woman into a modest, quiet, lovable woman, to be protected and cared for, appealing to all that is chivalrous in her menfolk, her very weakness her greatest strength.

CHAPTER XVI

WHEN CHINESE WOMEN DIE

IN a country where the worship of ancestors plays such an important part in the religion, death has a greater meaning than it has for those of Western lands. The Chinese spend far too much upon the ceremonies connected with death, rich and poor alike vying with each other in the elaborate arrangements for the disposal of their dead. I met not long ago the funeral procession accompanying the body of a captain of labour to his last resting-place. He was many times a millionaire, who began life as a boatman. The sons boasted that they spent twenty thousand dollars on his funeral. There were eight native bands in the procession, led by the European band of Shanghai, twenty men carrying banners and umbrellas, about fifty men carrying scrolls, on which were written the name and rank of the deceased; there were over two hundred Buddhist priests, dressed in their sackcloth robes, and the wailing mourners and friends in their mourning clothes of white, followed in sedan-chairs and carriages. The enormous coffin was covered with red embroidered satin and carried by thirty, chanting coolies. Within the home the walls were covered with white, and there were long scrolls from friends telling of their sympathy, and of the greatness of the deceased family. At twenty tables, seating eight each, feasting was carried on day and night for a week.

In the summer-time there are hundreds of deaths, and the funerals of the poor pass our house daily. They are very different from the elaborate processions of the rich men. The coffins, instead of being made of the finest teak or heaviest ebony, are nothing but plain, rough boxes, and the mourners either are on wheelbarrows or they walk to the place of the dead, the weeping wife being supported on each side by a friend, who practically carries her as she stumbles along in her grief. Paper money is always scattered in front of the corpse in order to pay his way into the new world; and often one sees either a live rooster or an imitation one standing on the coffin to bring back to his home one of the man's three souls.

The body is often kept months within the houses before a suitable day is found by, the necromancer on which to bury him, but because of the manner of preparing for burial it is not insanitary to keep a corpse in the house for a few months. The coffins are made of hardwood of four or five inches in thickness. First a certain number of bags of lime are placed in the bottom, varying according to the weight of the person ; over that is laid a wadded blanket, if of a rich family it is of silk and often embroidered, if the person be poor it is only cotton ; the body is laid in the coffin, dressed in as handsome a suit of wadded clothing as is consistent with the means of the family ; the ancestral tablet is laid upon the breast, paper money at the feet ; he is covered with the blanket and the coffin hermetically sealed. The coffin is the most precious possession of the Chinese, and is often purchased years before death in order that they may be sure of a dignified last resting-place.

We often hear stories told at women's clubs of mothers who throw babies within the " baby tower " to die. These baby towers are small, round houses, situated on the outskirts of a city or a village for the purpose of permitting the poor to dispose of their dead children without the expense of a coffin or a funeral. The interior of the house is partially filled with quicklime, and a small door opening on to a slanting chute permits the poor mother to give her baby its final resting-place. I have never heard of a case of a live baby being sent to these baby towers, as I found that a mother's heart is the same all over the world. My cook came to me one morning with his eyes red from weeping. I asked him the cause of his sorrow, and he told me that his three-months-old baby had died the evening before. He had no money with which to pay for its burial, so in the night, when the mother had at last fallen into a sleep, he softly arose and, wrapping the tiny body in a blanket, had laid it upon the table with twenty cents beside it in order that the garbage-man who came in the early morning might take it to the baby tower outside the city. I said to him : " But, cook, why did you not bury it properly? Does not your wife feel very badly? " He shook his head sorrowfully, and said : " Yes, she too muchee cry, but what can we do? We must buy rice for live babies." That is the great secret of the stoicism of the Chinese race. They must buy rice for the living, and what often seems to us as heartlessness and cruelty is simply the effect of the great economic pressure in a land where millions are on the verge of starvation, and where the lack of a day's work means the lack of a day's food.

In times of great epidemics rich Chinese and the guilds or clubs of different forms of industry, such as the Bankers' Guild, the Tea Guild, or the Goldsmiths' Guild, provide coffins for the burial of the poor, and in times of famine these same guilds are most generous to their less fortunate brothers. Near Soochow is a tomb of a man who gave his entire fortune to relieving the wants of the people of his province during a time of famine. He is buried in the most picturesque spot in the hills, the road to which is bordered

17

by a great many enormous boulders that rise
straight up from the ground. The Chinese say
that these stones stood up to show their
respect for the great man when his body
was carried to its last resting-place and that
they are waiting his commands to lie down
again.

The dead are buried on the family estate; if
there is not room for all, a spot is leased from
a neighbour. The interment is not beneath the
surface except in a few provinces; the coffin
is set on the ground and the dirt is heaped over
it. Sometimes the fields are so thickly covered
with mounds that there is little room left for
cultivation. Especially is this so in the country
around Shanghai, which looks to the casual
passer-by like one vast graveyard. Funeral
expenses for parents are the most sacred of
obligations, and it is not uncommon for the sons
to part with everything they have in the world in
order to render proper respect to the memory
of their parents. A son is supposed to mourn
three years for his father, during which time all
occupation is to cease. In the case of a son
holding an important official position, he often
has to resign his post during the period of mourning, or else be called unfilial. Strict mourning
for the mother only lasts three months, otherwise
the same honour is paid her memory as given
to the head of the household.

When a woman is left a widow, she often vows
that she will not remarry, and she spends her life

in pious acts that cause her village or her clan at her death to erect a memorial to her honour. This is generally in the form of an arch, built of stone and erected near her village. In the country districts one can see many, of these concrete evidences of the respect which the Chinese have for loyal womanhood.

CHAPTER XVII

CHANGING CHINA

CHINA is changing so rapidly, and is becoming so thoroughly Westernized, especially in the ports where the Chinese come in contact with the foreigner, that she can scarcely be recognized by her old-time friends. We all admit that the change is for the better so far as the nation is concerned, but whether it makes for the individual good is another and more serious question. China is flooded with foreign adventurers who want her untouched wealth, and who have cast their greedy eyes upon her mines of coal and iron and gold. These foreigners from all classes and grades of society have brought dishonesty and corruption in business dealings to the merchant of China, whose word in the old time was as good as his bond. In those days when a Chinaman said, " Can putee book," it was known that the contract was settled and that he would live up to his spoken word, whether it meant loss or profit to him. But when dealing with the foreigner the Chinese found that there

RICE-BOATS ON CANAL, CHINA.

To face p. 262.

were no old-time customs to bind the merchant from over the seas, except those of bond and written agreement. If he had any traditions of honour, he evidently left them in the homeland, as nothing less than a court of law would hold him to his contract if it seemed expedient for him to break it.

For years the word " China " meant to the adventurer of other lands a place for exploitation, where money was to be obtained easily by the man with fluent tongue and winning ways. Even foreign officials did not scruple to use their influence to enter trade. In one of the great inland cities there was no water nearer than a river several miles away. A foreign official, boring an artesian well upon his place and finding pure, clear water, conceived the idea of boring wells throughout the city and bringing water to the doors of the half-million of people who resided in its narrow streets. He interested the officials and raised a sum of money, and to doubly assure the Chinese that their money was safe he signed the contracts, not only with his name but affixed to them the great seal of his Government. After a few months' trip to his homelands, and a few aimless borings in the earth in search of the water that never came, he relinquished the project, but not the money, and the officials could do nothing but gaze sadly into the great holes that had taken their silver. They learned that wisdom comes with experience and now put into practice the proverb : " When a man has been burned once with hot soup, he for ever afterwards blows upon cold rice."

Another case in which the Chinese officials were duped by clever-tongued foreigners was in Ningpo. Three Americans visited that city and talked long and loud of the dark streets, the continual fires caused by the flickering lamps of oil that were being constantly overturned by the many children. They showed the officials the benefits of electricity, that a light upon each corner would make it impossible for robbers and evildoers to carry on their work, which must be done in darkness. They promised to turn night into day, to give poor as well as rich the incandescent lamp at no greater cost than the bean-oil wick. They were most plausible, and raised thirty thousand dollars as contract money. They left, ostensibly to buy machinery; the years have passed; they never have returned. Ningpo still has streets of darkness, men still walk abroad with lighted lanterns, the lamp is seen within the cottage, and will continue to be quite likely until the hills shall fade, if electricity depends upon the officials who once dreamed dreams of a city lit by a light from Western lands.

This is one of the most serious handicaps of the missionary in trying to Christianize China. The dissolute white man is in every port, manifesting a lust, greed, and brutality which the Chinese, who are accustomed to associate the citizenship of a person with his religion, attribute to Christianity. It is no wonder that it is

hard for the missionary to make converts among
the people who have business dealings with men
from Christian nations.

But there are other questions besides those of
business integrity vitally affecting the Chinese
youth to-day. Along with the slight knowledge
which they have obtained of the manners and
customs of the Western world, they have absorbed
many of its vices. With their rose-wine and their
samshu the Chinese boy has learned to drink
champagne and brandy. I know the father of
five sons who told me that he would give all
that he possessed in the world if he had not
brought those sons to Shanghai.

Change is now the order of the day in China,
educationally as well as politically. We do not
hear the children shouting their tasks at the top
of their little voices, nor do they learn by heart
the thirteen classics. The simple schoolroom,
with hard benches and earthen floor, with a faint
light striking through the unglazed windows, is
no more. The old-time examinations at Peking
have gone, the degrees which have been the
nation's pride have been abolished, the subjects
of study in the schools have been completely
changed. The privileges which were once given
the scholars, the social and political offices which
were once open to the winners of the highest
prizes, have been thrown upon the altar of
modernity. The faults of the old system of
education lay in the stress it placed upon
the memorizing of the many books whose con-

tents were not always understood by the young
mind, and in the lack of original ideas that might
be expressed by a student, who must give the
usual interpretation of the classics. Now the
introduction of free thought and private opinion
has produced an upheaval in the minds of China's
young men, and they say what they think, even
trying to show that Confucius was at heart a
staunch Republican, and that Mencius only thinly
veiled his sentiments of modern philosophy. It
is generally conceded that the newer education
leads to the greater individualism which is now
the battle-cry of China.

The Chinese, both men and women, are reaching out eager hands to obtain for themselves the
knowledge that is being brought from other
lands. Yet this thirst for education is not a
newly acquired virtue, for in no country is real
learning held in higher esteem than in China.
It is the greatest characteristic of the nation that
in every grade of society education is considered
above all else. As a race they have devoted
themselves to the cultivation of literature for a
longer period by some thousands of years than
any existing nation. To literature, and to it alone,
they look for the rule to guide them in their
conduct. To them all writing is sacred, and the
very symbols and materials used in the making
of the written character have become objects of
veneration. Even the smallest village is provided with a scrap-box, into which every bit of
paper containing printed or written words is care-

fully placed, to await a suitable occasion when it may be burned.

The mission schools have been the pioneers in the education of the young people of China, and if the teaching of Christianity has not as yet made many converts, the effect has been great in the spread of higher ideals of education, and much of the credit of the progress of the modern life of China to-day must be given to the mission schools, which have opened new pathways in the field of learning and caused the youth of China to demand a higher system of education throughout the land.

It is said that practically all the officials in the new China are men who have been educated abroad or who have been in one of the many mission schools scattered throughout the country. They are the ones who have taken what they have learned of foreign lands and adapted it to the needs of their country ; but there are others who have been abroad only long enough to acquire the veneer of Western education, and they are the young men who become the discontented ones of China.

When Chinese boys go to a foreign land they have many difficulties to overcome. They must receive their information and instruction in a language not their mother tongue. They have small chance to finish their education by practical work in bank or shop or factory. They get a mass of book knowledge and little opportunity to practise the theories that they learn, and they are not clever enough to understand that their textbook knowledge is nearly all foreign to their country and to the temperament of their race. When they return to their home they often find that they have grown out of touch with their people's ways and customs. They come back looking for employment, for a chance to use their new-found knowledge ; but they feel that they should begin at the top of the ladder instead of working up slowly rung by rung, as their fathers did before them. They feel that they are entitled to be masters, not realizing that even with this wonderful foreign education acquired, experience is necessary to make them leaders of great enterprises or of men. It is these boys who are the teashop orators and preach the Socialistic dogma for which China will not be prepared for many years to come.

The Chinese boys and girls are going too far and too fast in their thirst for the broader knowledge and teaching of the Western world. It is like the clothes that the Chinese girl is wearing, trying to imitate her sisters of the Occident. She has discarded the soft, clinging silks, the gay embroideries, the jade and flowers in her black locks, for the straight, dark skirt, the ugly coats, and the untidy manner of dressing the hair seen with the European women of the coast towns. These do not become her, any more than the scientific degrees become the woman who has been for centuries a woman of the·home. We do not condemn education for the Chinese woman any more than we entirely condemn the change in the style of clothing ; but they should both be adapted to the individual. This new education seems to be too general, the personality of the boy or girl being entirely left out. The youth are being made into a set of jelly-moulds, all looking alike, all trying to be formed upon the models brought them from England or America.

Three things should be taken into account— who the boy or girl is, where he is, and where he is going. The mistake should not be made in China that has been made in India—that is, the turning out of a race of barristers and clerks from her schools. China needs technical schools for her boys and common sense applied to the education of her girls. I have been in a school for the education of the daughters of the better class of Chinese, where the main accomplishment for which the girl was applauded was her facility in rendering a piece upon the piano. I should have said " executing " a piece upon the piano, because that is exactly what is done when a Chinese girl attempts to inter- pret foreign music. It is alien to her in every way, and generations of study will not make the Chinese maiden a musician in the foreign sense, nor will they really care for the foreign music. These girls who have wasted so many hours in the practise of the piano will go to homes where they cannot have a piano, or if they did have one they would be the only persons in the family who would appreciate its music. It would be a conglomeration of bad sounds to father, mother, husband. Many feel that the young girls would be better employed in learning a musical instrument understood and appreciated by her people and one that would give pleasure to her husband at night, and perhaps be a factor in keeping him from the tea-house, and the singing-girls who have a monopoly of the musical talent of China.

Another thing that causes sorrow to the conservative fathers and mothers is the fact that as soon as their children receive a smattering of the Western civilization they immediately begin to scoff at their own modes of acquiring knowledge and the textbooks which have trained their people's minds for so many years. They become proud of the fact that they know nothing of the classics, and they quote Shelley, Byron, Burns, and Browning instead of their own beautiful poets. But, what is more serious for the youth of this Eastern land, this worldly knowledge seems to have freed his intelligence without teaching him self-control, and it has taken him away from the gods of his fathers without replacing them with others. He, like his cousin of Japan, is inclined to become agnostic and say, " There are no gods."

Whether the religion from the West is the religion best suited for the Oriental we cannot say, but whatever he receives from us must be adapted to fit the needs and conditions of his race and country. China must raise up leaders from her own people, both men and women, as her regeneration will come from within, not without. More and more the West must see that the East and the West may meet, but they can never mingle. Foreigners can never enter the inner door of Chinese thought or feeling. The door is never wholly opened, the curtain never quite drawn aside between the two races. They are unlike in almost every characteristic. The Westerner is much more a materialist than is the cultured man of China. To him the taste of the tea is not so important as the aroma, and the acquiring of wealth and honours is not so much to be desired as is the ability to live the leisured life, the life of thought and meditation, when he may sit apart from the noise and cares of the present day.

The rush and worry of the Western world seem to have penetrated even to the women's courtyard, and there is no doubt that the new China will be Westernized in every department of her being. But we who love China hope that she will not change too rapidly, that she will take what is necessary for her happiness from the knowledge and the mode of life of the Occident, but that she will touch it with her own individuality, making it a real part of her and not simply becoming an imitation of the alien people by whom she is surrounded.

There is a charm about old China, and there is more than a charm about the old-time secluded Chinese women, who have been protected and guarded from life's worries and battles, until they represent all that is most beautiful and feminine and demand the chivalry of the men of the world.

Let the West come to China with all its modern inventions and its politics and educational policies, but let us always be able to find within its quiet courtyards the quiet, sweet-faced woman of China.

CHAPTER XVIII

JAPANESE WOMEN AT HOME

I HAVE been eight times to Japan, living in the big European hotels in Yokohama, Tokio, Kobe, and Nagasaki, stopping for days at a time in the native inns in the interior, or visiting at the homes of friends. I decided that my ninth trip to the little island would be different; consequently we planned a few months' stay in some out-of-the-way place where we could keep house and live *à la Japonaise*. We had heard of the beauties of Hakodate, the most northern port of any size in Japan, and obtaining a letter to the American Consul, we wrote him asking if it were possible for him to find us a furnished Japanese house for the summer months. We were delighted to hear a few days later that he had found a place for us, the summer home of a rich merchant, situated on the mountain-side, overlooking the sea, and surrounded by giant cryptomerias and pines. Needless to say, we were soon on our way to this paradise.

There were only four berths in the sleeping-car on the Northern Express, and we engaged two, but were not given the opportunity of using them. At one of the stations a prince with his retinue came on the train and pre-empted the entire car. He used only one of the berths, as no one could sleep over him, nor evidently near him, and on all the long journey he selfishly occupied the room by himself, while we, in company with the half-dozen men composing his suite, had to fit ourselves into a tiny compartment that should have only accommodated four. The men removed their elaborate outer robes, curled themselves into comfortable positions, and smoked and chatted or slept until a station of any importance was neared, when they donned their gowns, threw around their necks a long, stiff piece of silk on which was embroidered the Imperial chrysanthemum, and prepared to receive the delegation of townspeople who were always at the station to present an address to his Imperial Highness, or to send in an elaborate meal, served on beautifully lacquered trays.

I had a good look at the prince on his entrance, and found him exactly like the representations of the daimios of olden times that we see on the fans and tea-boxes. He had the long, slim, pale face of the aristocrat, absolutely different from the round-faced Japanese who comprise the greatest proportion of the island's population. He looked as if he might almost belong to another race. I was told by one of his men that he represented to many thousands of the people a god, as in his branch of the family a certain godhead had descended from father to son. When the train stopped for any length of time at a station, the people came in crowds and knelt, touching their heads to the ground, and one old lady kept bowing and holding up her hands, with the tears streaming down her face at the joy of beholding so great a divinity. He looked at them without seeing them at all, never showing by any motion or sign that there was anything to be seen except the distant hills. I do not see how it was possible for any human being to look so thoroughly impersonal at a crowd of bowing, worshipping people, when he knew he was the object of all the adoration. Yet he looked at them as if their faces were windows and their back hair the landscape.

Train travel is interesting in Japan, if one will travel in the ordinary day coach and watch the people. The Japanese are great travellers, and the clack-clack of their wooden clogs makes a deafening noise at the stations, especially on the bridges leading over the tracks. One sees whole families going for an outing or on a visit to a distant relative. They come on the train with bundles and packages—most mysterious things done up in large squares of cloth. They drop their shoes before the seat and curl their feet under them, and proceed thoroughly to enjoy themselves. The seats run lengthwise of the cars, and often a little woman gets tired of looking out of the windows or at her fellow-passengers opposite, and, turning her back on the car and sitting practically upright, will lean her face against the side of the window and go to sleep. The manner in which they can sit upon their feet for hours impresses a foreigner. At the larger stations tea in tiny pots, with a little porcelain cup, is brought in by the salesmen, and " bento," the lunch of cold rice, pickles, and fish of some description, is sold in neat boxes, the dainty lunch only costing ten cents, including a pair of new wooden chop-sticks. The Japanese masses, like their prototypes everywhere, enjoy eating in public, and the car is filled with the divers and sundry odours of fruit, sweets, tea, and food. They are not noisy, and always most polite, and because of the dainty clothes of the women and children, and the variety of their colouring, a few hours can be spent quite well in studying travelling Japanese close at hand. At one station a party of pilgrims came on, dressed in white. They belonged to some club in a far northern village whose members paid a small assessment each week, and each year lots were chosen to judge who should benefit by the annual pilgrimage to some famous shrine or to Mount Fuji. The lucky winners in the lottery joined other pilgrims, donned the pilgrim's dress, and under the direction of a guide made the one great visit of their lives, the wonders of which they would be able to tell their amazed neighbours when they returned. These would listen with interest, as it might be their good fortune to draw the lucky number the coming year.

At the end of our long train ride, Amorri, we went on the small boat bound for Hakodate, where we were met by the Consul, a jolly, big, whole-hearted man, who took us, metaphorically speaking, at once to his bosom and became as a long-lost brother. His wife, much to our surprise, was a tiny little Japanese woman, no bigger than a good-sized doll, and as pretty as a picture. They looked so incongruous together that one was inclined to smile. He weighed at least 250 lb., was over six feet tall; and I should think that when dressed in all her finery, Mrs. Consul might have weighed 85 lb. She was a well-educated, well-informed little woman, who needed all her charm and tact to keep her unruly family in order. It was a big one, the last, a boy, being the pride of the father's heart, and as nearly spoiled as the clever mother would allow him to be by his worshipping father. When I knew them better it was a joy to me to see how she managed these children. The father, who had been at one time captain of a sailing vessel, always spoke to them as if they were at the top of a mast on a wintry night with a cyclone blowing. Tommy, the irrepressible, would get up on the window seat, and his father would hail him in a voice that could be heard by the boats coming from Kamschatka: "Tommy, get out of that window seat; you'll break your neck." Tommy would not move; again his father's stentorian tone would offend the evening air. The quiet little mother would turn and give a nod of her pretty head to Tommy, and Tommy would immediately climb down from his perch and proceed to behave himself as young boys should.

The Consulate was partly foreign and partly Japanese, and the children while at home in the morning dressed in kimona and wooden clogs, but in the afternoon they were gay in " home " dresses and resplendent in hair ribbons, only showing by the little turn of the eyes that they were members of their mother's race.

Soon after our arrival we went to see the place that was to be our home for the next few months. We did not see the house until we came to the great gateway with its pointed roof leading into a path shaded by giant cryptomerias, completely guarding the house from view of the passer-by. This hillside garden contained about five acres of land, in which were winding pathways, giant pine-trees, terraces of flowers, and here and there a tori, a huge bronze stork, a grim stone lantern, or a calmly reposing Buddha to show us we were in the land of Nippon. We looked out over the northern ocean, dotted here and there with the sails of fishing-boats, or saw the smoke of a steamer coming from Kamschatka, Saghlain, or some of those mysterious northern ports, the names of which were only places on a map. After listening for awhile to the murmur of the surf, we visited the interior of the house, which contained five rooms. The furniture consisted of the matting on the floor, the sliding " shojis,"

JAPANESE CHILDREN PLAYING.

To face p. 276.

the fire-boxes, the cooking utensils, and dishes
for the serving of the meals. It was necessary
for us to buy our " futons "—that is, our bedding ;
but otherwise the home was completely furnished
à la Japonaise. The servant problem was easily
solved, as the daughter of the gardener wished
to be our maid, the gardener would run our
errands, and his wife would be the general super-
intendent of the place. I expected to do the
cooking, as the time would be too short in Hakodate to train a man in matters culinary. We
were soon installed, and then passed pleasant
days in *dolce far niente*, spending our mornings
in trips to the seashore, watching the fishermen
come in with their boatloads of squids. Their
arrival was the signal for all the women and
children of the village to flock to the shore and
unload the boats, then, after cleaning and pressing these ugly fish, hang them upon lines to dry,
making the whole ocean front as far as the eye
could see a miniature wash-Monday. We were
not allowed to climb the mountain-sides except
to a certain distance, as the hills were heavily
fortified, and at sudden turns we were met by
great signs which stated plainly in English,
French, German, Japanese, and Russian that
further explorations were forbidden. We never
tried to disobey the laws in Japan, as these little
people are vigorous in their punishment of offen-
ders, to whatever race they may belong, and I
feel that they have been justified in upholding the
manhood of their people. In India and in China

you see the white man treat the native with bar-
barous cruelty. While travelling once in India
our servant was making up the bed in the compartment we had engaged on the train. A white
man entered, and without one word of explana-
tion, grabbed our man and beat and kicked him
and nearly threw him out of the car. In reply to
our indignant demands as to the cause of his
ill-treatment of our servant, he said that he
thought the man had made a mistake in the
berth and was taking one for which he had paid.
I said afterward to Ali, " Why did you not strike
him when he treated you so brutally?" Ali
replied : " Oh, mem-sahib, he was a white man.
If I had touched him I would have lain many
long days in prison." In China also, on one hot
day in August I saw a rickshaw coolie, naked to
the waist, with the perspiration running down his
face in streams, running swiftly with a heavy
man inside his two-wheeled carriage. In passing by a crowded corner, he brushed against
a white man, who was having his afternoon stroll.
The white man angrily turned, and, grabbing the
coolie by his hair, beat him across his bare back
with his cane until he stopped from sheer ex-
haustion. The panting, perspiring coolie was
helpless as he could not drop the shafts, and so
was compelled to take the punishment. His
patron in the carriage, a richly-dressed Chinese,
dared not interfere because he also was a native
and understood there was no court of justice
when it was a question of a white man's word

against that of the yellow man. They have a
saying in China, that when a Chinese walks along
the sidewalk of his own city of Shanghai, he is
pushed into the middle of the road by the American, who only laughs at him, by the Englishman,
who swears at him, and by the German, who
kicks him, but—he is pushed into the middle of
the road. This could not happen in Japan, as
the Japanese courts punish severely any one who
dares to lay his hand in violence upon a Japanese,
however lowly may be his station or however
strong may be the provocation. While we were
in Yokohama, an officer of an American ship had
his hand severely hurt through the carelessness of
a Japanese longshoreman. In his pain and first
flush of anger he knocked the Japanese down,
and for his impatience was compelled to remain
six months in jail. His captain and his Consul
tried their best to help him, but it was in vain,
and he saw his ship sail away without him.

I came very near sharing his fate while in
Hakodate. The fisherman came to our doors each
morning with his enormous baskets of fish swung
over his shoulders. The maid, her mother, and
myself, spent many interesting moments in turning over the scaly contents of his baskets in
order to make our choice amongst the varied
assortment he had for sale. I paid him by the
week, and one morning was called to the kitchen
by an indignant maid, who said the fisherman had
greatly overcharged me. The amount was far
too small, it seemed to me, to cause such keen

excitement, and I intended to dismiss the man, saying I would pay him, but employ him no more. I went over to a bucket of water, and taking up the long-handled dipper to take a drink, and not noticing that it was broken, I gave it a little shake toward the fisherman, and said, " Oh, go away, and don't make so much noise." The cup part of the dipper flew off and hit the indignant fisherman in the eye, whereupon he immediately shouldered his baskets and started for the magistrate. Needless to say, I was frightened, and I immediately donned my bonnet and started for the Consulate. The Consul heard my story and sadly shook his head : " If you really hit that coolie and he has you arrested, I can do nothing. It will only make matters worse to have me to interfere, so the best thing for you to do is to go with me and find that fisherman ; offer him half of your estate, but don't get mixed up with the law in Japan." For two hours we haunted side-streets, where at last we found our man, and, after a small money payment and a promise to take fish from him for the rest of the season, and practically binding myself to listen to his insolence as long as I was in Hakodate, he grudgingly assented to withdraw his charge.

These itinerant dealers make housekeeping in Japan easy. Men clad in blue cotton coats with great straw hats on their heads and baskets piled high with vegetables, come to the door each morning ; one passing along the streets both

night and day can hear the cries of the
travelling vendors, selling all that the average
householder may require.

Hakodate is filled with crows—monstrous,
black, impertinent thieves, who will come boldly
into the kitchen and take the fish from out the
frying-pan. Mornings I would take a pan of
corn, and in the rear of the house upon the hillside, and hitting upon the pan's side with a spoon,
would soon be surrounded by hundreds of these
beady-eyed birds, that are almost considered
sacred in this province. They were so tame that
they would fight at my feet for the kernels, and
I would be compelled to push them from my lap
and then, much to the maid's disgust, the greedy
birds would follow me into the house.

We used to play a game, the crows and I. I
would pound on the pan until I had summoned
fifty or sixty, then I would start the song,
" Onward, Christian Soldiers," and rapping on the
pan for accompaniment, would march solemnly
at the head of my serious, expectant army, up
hill and down dale, through the house, out again,
down the small paths, until even the maid who
considered the crows her enemies, would be compelled to laugh.

Soon I found that if I was to live as
the Japanese, I certainly should dress in the
clothes of the country, as European clothes and
shoes are not comfortable in Japanese houses.
All my friends were Japanese, and I found I
must conform to their customs so far as was pos-

sible if I would be happy and not an object of curiosity. Consequently I went with the wife of our Consul and passed two delightful hours in choosing kimonas, which, if I had been allowed to exercise my taste, would have been far too gay for one of my years. I always associated kimonas with pinks and blues and riotous colours, but I found that, being a married woman, I must confine my choice of colours to greys and browns and soft-toned mauves. I could indulge my love for ornamentation in the obis, as these may be of stiff brocades in rose and gold, or purple and gold, or, in fact, any colour one may wish. I found also that the Japanese dress itself may not be expensive, but the price of the obis is ruinous to a small pocket-book. It is in these last articles of adornment that the Japanese lady spends her husband's money. She buys obis and puts them away in her treasure-chest, only bringing them to the light of day on occasions of festivity. The tying of the obi is by no means a simple process, and I could never learn its intricacies. The end must be of a certain length, the big bow must be just so correctly arranged or else it shows that one is not *à la mode*. My friends were always lengthening an end or tying a little tighter the roll that gave the obi the correct tilt at the back. I found it necessary to practise privately for several days walking in the clogs before I dared try them in public. The Japanese have three kinds of clogs —high ones raised by two pieces of wood three or

four inches from the ground and with a piece
of leather as a mud-guard for use in wet weather ;
another pair of dress clogs were necessary, with
the plain wooden sole covered with fine matting ;
and still another pair of sandals, which were for
use around the garden or in places that did not
necessitate rough walking. The two pieces of
cord that pass between the great and the first
toe, and by which the clog is held on the foot,
compelled me to wear the Japanese sock, which
is made of white cotton, like a mitten, the great
toe being separated from the rest of the foot.
These socks are short, only coming to the ankle,
and are fastened by two or three metal clasps.
The shoes are never worn in the house, always
being left at the doorways, the thick cotton sole
of the stocking protecting the foot. It would be
as insulting to walk on the clean matting of a
Japanese house as it would be to walk on the
snowy damask of your hostess's dining-table.
After a few falls and many awkward movements
I found the Japanese foot-covering most comfortable, the foot being absolutely free ; but I soon
learned that my American stride did not conform
to the close-fitting dress of the kimona, as with
it the feet should not be set apart and one should
slightly " toe in " in order that the folds of the
kimona do not fly open. In one way Japanese
dress is not expensive, as the Japanese lady,
whatever her rank or wealth, does not wear
jewellery—no necklaces, nor bracelets, nor ear-
rings, nor brooches ; even rings are an in-

novation brought in with foreigners. Her only
jewels are the clasp of her obi fastener, generally
a piece of chased gold, and a couple of ornamental hairpins or a comb for the hair.

I did not attempt the hair-dressing, as that is
a most complicated affair, and must be left to
the attentions of a hair-dresser, who comes to the
homes once or twice a week and makes the
elaborate coiffures that add so much to the beauty
of a Japanese face. Each age has its coiffure,
and a woman never tries to disguise her age in
Japan, because by her dress and style of hair-
dressing she frankly confesses the stage she has
reached in life. There is the baby with her
shaven head, then the little queue tied on the
crown ; afterward the hair is cut square across the
neck, like the little dolls we see in the London
shops ; then when she is ten years old the hair
is divided and made into a bow knot tied with a
piece of ornamental paper. As she arrives at
young ladyhood there is the elaborate " shimada,"
which in the case of the young woman is very
large, and, if Nature has not been generous,
helped out with tresses bought in the shops. The
married woman has a special coiffure which
grows smaller with age, until, when she is a
matron of forty, the age when the woman of the
Orient considers herself an old woman, it is quite
small. If the woman is so unfortunate as to
lose her husband, she cuts her hair, and thus
shows all the world that she is a widow. The
Japanese mature early, and old age comes to

them sooner than it does to people from the West. A Japanese proverb says that man lives but fifty years, and rarely does his span exceed seventy years. In former days old age began at fifty, and a man then considered himself unfit for business and made over his name and property to his son, passing the rest of his life in ease without the cares of business. Old age is not a burden to the Japanese woman, but is a paradise to be looked for longingly. Then she, who has perhaps been subservient to the mother of her husband all her married life, knows that she will be the head of her household, with her sons and daughters ready to obey her, and, because of her age and motherhood, respected and holding a position in life denied her as a young woman.

Many of these quiet, soft-voiced mothers of Japan were brought to call upon me by Mrs. Consul. They taught me how to serve the tea, the proper way of bowing, and even tried to make of me a good follower of the Law by taking me with them to the temples and visiting shrines and holy places. One kindly woman brought me a tablet for my " august-spirit-dwelling," which she placed in a tiny model of a Shinto temple and put above the inner doorway of the hall, where I was supposed to burn before it each morning candles and incense, and keep the little cups for rice and water filled. I was well provided with gods, as another friend gave me a Buddha for my household shrine, and all the paraphernalia of service with which to worship him.

Below us on the hillside was the swagger tea-house of the town, and the tinkle of the samisens and the singing of the pretty girls came to us faintly until late into the night. This pretty music, mingled with the sound of the surf upon the shore, was always the last sound we heard at night after the maid had placed the night-light, the tobacco-box, and the brazier for the tea at our head, and then had knelt and said " Good-night." In the morning we were wakened by a softly murmured " O Hayo," and a tray of tea was respectfully slid across the matting to give us strength to begin the morning's work.

While in Hakodate I made the acquaintance of many Japanese ladies and learned their customs and the manner of their life, which is controlled by thoughts and ideals entirely different from those entertained by women of the Western world. I think I much prefer the woman of the old school, with her charming manners, her elaborate bows, and her antiquated superstitions and beliefs, to her daughter, who, like her sister of China, India, and Egypt, is trying too hard to wear clothes not made for her, and to adapt customs and usages for which she is not formed temperamentally or physically. The customs of the modern world will come to the woman of Japan, but they must be adapted to her conditions and not be taken *en masse*.

One of the most beautiful characteristics of the Japanese is their reverence for old age and their intense love for children. Japan has justly been called the baby's paradise, and certainly in no country does the home life so thoroughly revolve around the children as it does in Japan. Like all Eastern women, the desire for children is the most ardent wish of the Japanese woman's heart. The childless wife will move heaven and earth in her desire to gain the blessing of motherhood. She will visit watering-places, offer prayers at temples, make long, irksome pilgrimages, wear amulets, drink strange decoctions, and allow herself to be imposed upon and robbed by every charlatan who claims a knowledge that will help her gain the craving of her heart—a child. It will, therefore, be imagined with what eagerness the arrival of a little stranger is awaited in the home, and the happiest day in the girl-wife's life is the day on which they tell her she is the mother of a son.

As soon as the event takes place, a special messenger is dispatched to notify friends and relatives while letters of announcement are sent to those who are not so closely related in friendship to the family. All thus notified must then make a visit to the new baby and either send or bring with them a present. Toys or clothing, always accompanied by eggs or a fish to bring good luck, come in great profusion, and when baby is about thirty days old, return presents must be made to all who remembered him at time of birth. When baby is seven days old he receives his name, and when he is thirty-one—or if a girl, when she is thirty-three—days old, the first important occasion of his life must be observed. He is dressed in his best and gayest garments, and, accompanied by members of his family, is taken to a temple and placed under the protection of one of the Shinto deities, who is supposed to become the guardian of the child through life. This is a day for present-giving also, and one especial gift must come to the child, a papier mâché dog, which is always placed at the head of the child's bed at night as a charm against evil influences.

The infant should not walk until it is a year old ; but if it is so precocious that it commences to toddle before that time, a small bag of rice is laid upon its back, and it is made to stumble and fall. To walk before its first birthday is a sign that it will die young or else become a resident of a distant land. There are many superstitions connected with the early life of a baby. If he sucks his fingers before he does his thumb, he will be a help to his parents in their old age. If he crawls out of his covers at night, he will rise in the world, but if he snuggles down in the bed and is inclined to crawl towards the foot, it augurs that a downward course is his fate in life. If many of the children of a family have died in infancy, the nervous mother will make for this last gift of the gods a dress composed of thirty-three pieces of cloth collected from thirty-three different families, or she will shave his head until he is seven years old, or give him a girl's name instead of a boy's, thus deceiving the gods who covet her treasure. If baby has prickly heat, the first egg plant of the season is hung over the door ; while suspending the empty rice-pot, still hot, over the baby's head for a few moments will make him immune from that afflic-tion of childhood, the measles. It passes its days tied to the back of little brother or sister or nurse until it can walk, then when it is two years old the fifteenth of November is a great day for all the babies. They are taken to the temple and the blessing of the gods is invoked, and the priests purify their bodies by waving over them a sacred wand. This is the occasion for showing new clothes and calling upon all friends, who make presents to the child.

At three or four years children are sent to a kindergarten, and at six years they enter the Primary Schools, where there is a six-years' com-pulsory course for both boys and girls. Then it only rests with the parents whether the child receives a higher education, as there are in all towns and villages a Middle School for boys and a High School for girls. The average girl stops her education with the Primary School, or at most with the High School, but there is a University in Tokio where the girl may complete her edu-cation and fit herself for a vocation. But if she has been six years at Primary School and four years at High School, she is sixteen years old, and of a marriageable age, although the average girl does not marry until she is eighteen or nine-teen.

There are a great many accomplishments

19

which it is necessary for a Japanese girl of good
family to know. The knowledge of needlework
is so general that it really is not considered an
accomplishment. But the art of letter-writing
must be known by all accomplished young ladies,
and the tea ceremony, which is the strictest
and most complicated of all the ceremonies
which surround the cultured Japanese, must be
thoroughly learned by the daughter of the house.
Each movement is regulated by custom, and a
mistake in turn of hand or position of the body
or the omission of any of the minute details in
regard to the bows and salutations in offering,
receiving, and returning the cups would show a
lack of proper training. The young girl is taught
the arrangement of flowers, which is an art by
itself in Japan. In the sitting-room of a
Japanese home there is a single vase of flowers
sitting in the tiny alcove, and they would lose
half of their attraction if they were not in some
manner symbolical in tone and colour with the
picture upon the kakemono which hangs above
them. The young girl is often taught to play
upon the koto, a kind of zither, although the
national musical instrument is the samisen, which
is played everywhere—at home, in story-tellers'
halls and theatres, and at every tea-house party.
Girls start to learn this instrument at a very early
age, because it is necessary to learn it while the
fingers are still pliant. It takes time to learn
these instruments, as there are no scores and the
tunes must be committed to memory. Women

AN OUTDOOR KITCHEN IN JAPAN.

To face p. 290.

teachers come to the home to teach the girls in
all these arts, and often the samisen teacher has
been a famous geisha, whose support now is
teaching the music that once made her welcome
at the dinner-parties of gay Japan.

After mastering the accomplishments, her
business in life is now to marry, and few Japanese
maidens think seriously of any other lot in life
than that of marrying and becoming the mothers
of future Japanese. Japan is more progressive
than any other Oriental country, if we except
Burmah, in that it allows the girl to exercise a
certain amount of choice in the selection of a
husband. There are never cases of love matches,
but if she positively objects to a man who is
proposed to her, she is seldom forced to marry
him. It would be thought most immodest if
she refused to marry a man until she loved him,
as love is supposed to come with marriage and
the advent of the children. Only simple tolera-
tion is expected before the marriage. The offices
of a go-between are asked to assist in the search
for a husband or wife, unless the match is made
by friends of the interested parties. When the
future husband has been selected, the go-
between, who must always be a married man, as
his wife takes an important part in the transac-
tions, brings about a meeting of the young couple
as if by accident. They may be strolling in a
garden looking at the hanging wistaria, or meet at
a theatre, where the families are introduced, and
the two most concerned have a chance to take

a good look at each other, and the next day, when
the anxious match-maker comes to the house to
learn whether his choice has met with favour,
they will give their consent, or the match will be
broken off, and the go-between will start again
the hunt for an eligible alliance. If everything
is satisfactory, a lucky day is appointed for the
formal proposal, presents are exchanged, and
then all look forward to the wedding. A couple
of days before the wedding the bride's trousseau
and household gods are sent to her new home,
and its elaborateness is only limited by the
father's wealth. Yet there are some things considered indispensable in the outfit of a bride,
such as a bureau, a writing-table, a work-box,
two of the little trays on which meals are served,
together with the full dining outfit, and two or
more complete sets of bed furnishings. If she
is of a rich family, quite likely the clothing she
will bring with her will last her entire life, as
styles do not change so radically as to make
gowns go so completely out of fashion that
they cannot be worn. A wedding is a most expensive proceeding for the father of the bride,
as each member of the groom's family—father,
mother, brothers, sisters, aunts, and cousins,
even the servants—must all receive a present to
mark the joyous occasion. The wedding itself
is in the presence of only a few witnesses, and
consists in a few formal acts, the most important
of which is the drinking "three times three"
cups of saki together. To make the marriage

conform to the laws of Japan, the bride's name is removed from her family register and transferred to that of her husband's family.

After the ceremony there are entertainments in the new home and at the home of the bride's parents, and then the couple settle down into the married state for two or three months, when the ultra-smart give a series of entertainments to the friends who had no formal announcement of the marriage.

The young wife does not have the happiness of setting up an establishment of her own, but she must go to the home of her husband's father. The mother-in-law question is a very serious one in Japan, because she is absolutely the head of the household, and the young wife has to submit in all things to her mother-in-law's will. This is especially serious for the modern Japanese girl, who perhaps has been educated in the Government school, if she is compelled to go to the home of a conservative old-time woman. Naturally, the mother cannot understand why, the ideas with which she herself was brought up should not be good enough for the other, and finds fault with, what are in her eyes, outlandish ways introduced by the new regime. These conservative women are always loud in praise of the old state of things, and believe that the world is going to ruin, socially, morally, and physically, because of the innovations brought into their homes by their progressive sons and daughters.

In addition to the parents of her husband, the wife has to win the affection of his brothers, sisters-in-law, and sisters, and her life is often made intolerable by the envies, jealousies, and petty faultfindings of the many women beneath the new roof-tree. The patriarchal life prevails in Japan as in all Eastern countries, and the successful man finds he must support a crowd of less successful relatives, whose claims are not admitted by law, but whose appeals on the score of kinship cannot be ignored, as custom allows those related by blood or marriage to look for help to the least unfortunate among them. The new civil code forces the support of parents, brothers, sisters, and other near relatives upon the head of the household, in addition to that of his wife and children. Thus a man is handicapped in life and has to spend the money he might otherwise use in educating his children in the support of uncles, aunts, and cousins, and perhaps a host of his wife's relations. From the social point of view this is undoubtedly an excellent system, as it relieves the nation of the support of its poor, but it bears heavily upon the individual, and many a young man's ambition has been shattered and his road to success blocked by the sordid cares and petty troubles caused by the necessity of maintaining a large household.

The great authority on the conduct of women who marry was written by a Japanese scholar, based on the teaching of the Chinese sages. In it the wife is told she must give unconditional obedience to her husband, who is in every respect her superior and the absolute lord and master of her body and soul ; whatever he does is right and she may not even murmur. She occupies a position in her husband's household practically of an upper servant. She must not frequent public resorts, nor go sight-seeing with the wealth her husband may obtain, and until she is forty years old is not to be seen in company, but to remain at home attending to her household and her children. This sounds very well, but women are women the world over ; and although Japanese wives are gentle, docile, and obedient, yet they have a virility and strength of character that compel the respect of their husbands, and in their own domain their word is law.

In the olden time each Japanese girl was supposed to know the precepts contained in a book called " Greater Learning for Women," written by a famous scholar several hundred years ago. For nearly two hundred years it was one of the indispensable articles that a bride took with her to her new home, but the present modern Japanese maiden knows very little of the " Greater Learning." I am afraid, indeed, that she is more thoroughly conversant with a parody of these famous precepts, which has been written by a young man of modern Japan. This is so radical that it is forbidden in the libraries of the mission schools in the fear that the Japanese girl will imbibe too early

the tendencies fatal to the happiness of
the Eastern woman, as she takes her first step
from her secluded doorway into the path that
leads to the higher learning of the Western
world.

Japanese women are womanly, kindly, gentle,
and pretty, and perhaps they owe this gentle-
ness and courtesy to the precepts taught by their
old sages.

According to Shingoro Takaishi, in his
" Wisdom and Women of Japan," the famous
moralist left the following instructions to help
women in their perilous journey through life—

" Seeing that it is a girl's destiny, on reaching
womanhood, to go to a new home, and live in
submission to her father-in-law, it is even more
incumbent upon her than it is on a boy to receive
with all reverence her parents' instructions.
Should her parents, through their tenderness,
allow her to grow up self-willed, she will in-
fallibly show herself capricious in her husband's
house, and thus alienate his affection ; while, if
her father-in-law be a man of correct principles,
the girl will find the yoke of these principles
intolerable. She will hate and decry her father-
in-law, and the end of these domestic dissensions will be her dismissal from her husband's
house and the covering of herself with ignominy.
Her parents, forgetting the faulty education they
gave her, may, indeed, lay all the blame on
the father-in law. But they will be in error ;
for the whole disaster should rightly be

attributed to the faulty education the girl received from her parents.

" More precious in a woman is a virtuous heart than a face of beauty. The vicious woman's heart is ever excited ; she glares wildly around her, she vents her anger on others, her words are harsh and her accent vulgar. When she speaks it is to set herself above others, to upbraid others, to envy others, to be puffed up with individual pride, to jeer at others, to outdo others—all things at variance with the way in which a woman should walk. The only qualities that befit a woman are gentle obedience, chastity, mercy, and quietness.

" A woman has no particular lord. She must look to her husband as her lord, and must serve him with all worship and reverence, not despising or thinking lightly of him. The great lifelong duty of a woman is obedience.

" A woman shall be divorced for disobedience to her father-in-law or mother-in-law. A woman shall be divorced if she fail to bear children, the reason for this rule being that women are sought in marriage for the purpose of giving men posterity. A barren woman should, however, be retained if her heart be virtuous and her conduct correct and free from jealousy, in which case a child of the same blood must be adopted ; neither is there any just cause for a man to divorce a barren wife if he have children by a concubine. Lewdness is a reason for divorce. Jealousy is a reason for divorce.

Leprosy or any, like foul disease is a reason for divorce. A woman shall be divorced who, by talking overmuch and prattling disrespectfully, disturbs the harmony of kinsmen and brings trouble on her household. A woman shall be divorced who is addicted to stealing.

"All the 'Seven Reasons for Divorce' were taught by the sage. A woman once married and then divorced has wandered from the 'way,' and is covered with great shame, even if she should enter into a second union with a man of wealth and position.

"It is the chief duty of a girl living in the parental house to practise filial piety towards her father and mother. But after marriage her duty is to honour her father-in-law and mother-in-law, to honour them beyond her father and mother, to love and reverence them with all ardour, and to tend them with practise of every filial piety,. While thou honourest thine own parents, think not lightly of thy father-in-law. Never should a woman fail, night and morning, to pay her respects to her father-in-law and mother-in-law. Never should she be remiss in performing any tasks they, may require of her. With all reverence must she carry out, and never rebel against, her father-in-law's commands. On every point must she inquire of her father-in-law and mother-in-law, and abandon herself to their direction. Even if thy father-in-law and mother-in-law be pleased to hate and vilify thee, be not angry, with them,

and murmur not. If thou carry piety towards
them to its utmost limits, and minister to them
in all sincerity, it cannot be but that they will
end by becoming friendly to thee."

There is a sword of Damocles always hanging over the head of the Japanese woman—that
is, the fear of divorce. Among the higher
classes the dread of scandal and gossip serves
as a restraint upon the too free use of the
power of divorce, but even now one meets many
respectable and respected persons who, some
time in their life, have gone through such an
experience. Obtaining a divorce is not such a
complicated affair as it is in America. It
is enough that the parties agree to separate and
make a declaration, witnessed by two reputable
witnesses, at a local magistrate's office, and the
divorce takes place by mutual consent. As in
the case of marriage the consent of the parents
or guardians of a girl under twenty-five years
of age and a man who is under thirty must be
obtained, so this consent of parents or guardians
is necessary before a divorce may be granted.
Then the domicile of the wife is retransferred in
the books of the registrar from the domicile of
the family in which she was married to that
of her original family. If one of the parties
concerned refuse to give their consent to the
divorce an application is made to the courts.
There are several grounds upon which judicial
divorce is granted—first, for bigamy; secondly,
the wife may be divorced for adultery, but not

the husband, unless the crime has been committed with a married woman, when the unfaithful wife and her lover are liable to penal servitude for a term not exceeding two years, if the charge is brought by the outraged husband. The man cannot be punished alone; the woman must share his fate. As in many European countries, marriage is forbidden between the respondent and the co-respondent in a divorce case.

Another, and one of the chief causes for divorce in Japan, are the complications that naturally arise from the many people living in one house. Either party may seek divorce if ill-treated or insulted by the parents or grandparents of the other, and mothers-in-law, with their hard tongues and bitter words, are the frequent causes of separation of husband and wife. One provision of the law which serves to make most mothers endure any evil of their married life rather than sue for divorce is the fact that the children belong to the father, and the mother returns childless to her father's house. In this country, where the woman is economically dependent upon her men-folk, even if she were allowed to take the children, quite likely they would not be made welcome in a home where there are always too many mouths to feed; therefore the Japanese mother puts up with many brutalities and heartaches in order to keep with her the only bright things she has in life, her children.

The Japanese wife leads a very busy life. In all but the very wealthiest and most aristocratic families the wife and daughters do a large part of the housework. In a house with no furniture, no carpets, no pictures, no stoves or furnaces, no windows to wash, no latest styles to be imitated in the making of clothing, there is not so much work in the care of a house as there is in the Western world, where the rooms are filled with a multitude of unnecessary articles that seem only made to give toil to women. But because of the lack of conveniences it takes time to properly care for the rooms in a Japanese house. Every morning there are the beds to be rolled up and placed in the closets, the mosquito-nets to be taken down, the rooms to be swept, dusted, and aired ; and the veranda floor is polished several times a day as if it were a precious piece of silver. The cooking and washing of the dishes take a great deal of time, as the former is done over a tiny charcoal stove and the dishes are washed in cold water. There is not a moment of time that the wife is idle, as there is always the family sewing to be super-intended, the mats and cushions to be re-covered, the wadding to be renewed in the bed coverings and the winter kimonas. Many of the Japanese dresses must be taken to pieces whenever they are washed, and the wet breadths smoothed upon a board and placed in the sun to dry. The careful housewife makes over the older daughters' dresses for the younger daughters, and these clothes are washed, turned, dyed, and made over and over again so long as there is a shred of the original material left to work upon.

The Japanese believe that a woman passes through three critical stages in her journey through life. If she passes her nineteenth, her thirty-third, and her thirty-seventh years safely, she has a chance of living to a good old age and seeing her children and her grandchildren grow up around her. Her most critical year is her thirty-third, and not only this year itself, but the years immediately preceding and following are considered inauspicious. Consequently there are three years during which period women will refrain as much as possible from acts which may appear like tempting Providence. When a woman attains her sixtieth birthday it is an occasion for great festivities, when she invites all her friends to a dinner to celebrate this wonderful event. If a man or woman should have occasion to celebrate their seventieth birthday, they distribute among their friends and relatives large red and white cakes with the character signifying "longevity" written upon them, and with each increasing year the old man or woman gain in the respect of their community.

When the last illness comes to father and mother it would be considered most unfilial for any of the children not to be present at the parent's death-bed. When all is over the son or the wife wets his lips with water, and so universal is this custom that the expression " to wet the dying lips with water " has come to signify the tending of a patient in his last illness. One of the reasons why the Japanese believe that the wife should be younger than the husband is that she may be able to fulfil this last office for her loved one.

It is known that death is in the room by the placing upside down of a screen before the bed, and the quilt covering the body is reversed, the foot covering the dead man's breast. A white cloth is laid over the face, as its exposure would be an obstacle to the soul's journey on its road to the other world. Everything done for the dead is the reverse of that done for the living ; for example, in the tub for the last bath cold water is poured first, then hot water added until it is of the right temperature. The head is shaved by touching it with the razor in small patches instead of running it continuously as in life. The burial garment is made by two women relatives, sewing with the same piece of thread in opposite directions, and the kimona is folded from right to left instead of from left to right as a man would wear it ordinarily. Mittens, leggings, and sandals are worn, the sandals being tied on the foot with the heel in the place of the toe, to signify that the dead must not return, drawn back by the love of the world. Around the neck is suspended a bag of Buddhist charms, and a small coin, or picture of a coin, with which

to pay, the ferryman. If the wife dies, the
husband does not publicly mourn for her,
although her children do ; but if the husband
dies the wife should mourn the rest of her life,
and she often cuts off her long hair and places
it in the coffin of her husband, showing that
she resolves to be always faithful to his memory,.
In a child's coffin a doll is placed to keep the
child company on its first journey without mother
or father.   The last rite is to cover the body
with incense-powder or dried aniseed, and then
it is ready for the funeral ceremonies.

A funeral procession in Japan is an imposing
affair.   The corpse, in its palanquin or in the
modern hearse, is preceded by men carrying large
white lanterns on poles, bundles of flowers stuck
in bamboo pedestals, stands of artificial flowers,
and birds in enormous cages, which are set free
at the temples as an act of merit.   The priests,
friends, and relatives move slowly and sadly, to
the temple, in which there is a service, then
the bier is taken to the crematory by, the chief
mourner and the near relatives.   The ashes are
removed the next day to their permanent home
in the public crematorium or in the temple
burying-ground of the family,.

For fifty, days after the death incense and
lights are kept burning before the tablet of the
deceased at his late home, and prayers are offered
at the grave for the same length of time.   A
priest comes from the temple every seventh day
to offer incense and prayers with the sorrowing

family, who believe that for forty-nine days the spirit of their dead wanders in the dark space that lies between this world and the next. Every seventh day it makes a step forward and is helped by the prayers of loved ones left behind. The sorrowing wife is taught that the spirit cannot tear itself away from its old home and hovers over it, and unless it is absolutely necessary no loving woman would remove from her home until the forty-nine days were past, for fear of giving sorrow to the spirit of her husband, if he did not find her in the place where they had passed together their years of happiness.

The dead are not quickly forgotten in Japan. Memorial services take place the forty-eighth day, the hundredth day, and the first anniversary of the death, and services are held for even fifty years. Lafcadio Hearn expresses the reverence which these people give their loved ones who have gone before them by saying :—

" In this worship we give the dead they are made divine. And the thought of this tender reverence will temper with consolation the melancholy that comes with age to all of us. Never in our Japan are the dead too quickly forgotten ; by simple faith they are still thought to dwell among their beloved and their place within the home remains holy. When we pass to the land of shadows we know that loving lips will nightly murmur our names before the family shrine, that our faithful ones will beseech us in their pain and bless us in their joy. We will not be left alone upon the hillside, but loving hands will place before our tablet the fruit and flowers and dainty food that we were wont to like, and will pour for us the fragrant cup of tea or amber rice-wine. Strange changes are coming upon this land, old customs are vanishing, old beliefs are weakening, the thoughts of to-day will not be the thoughts of to-morrow; but of all this we will know nothing. We dream that for us as for our mothers the little lamps will burn on through the generations; we see in fancy the yet unborn, the children of our children's children, bowing their tiny heads and making the filial obeisance before the tablet that bears our family name."

CONCLUSION

THE ocean that geographically divides the East from the West is not more wide nor deep than is that invisible ocean between the minds of the woman of the Orient and the woman of the Occident. A sympathetic understanding between peoples whose ideals have been so differently constructed, and who have had such radically opposite training, is next to impossible. No matter what the Western woman may do in the hope of touching the emotional life of the woman of the East, she soon finds that further progress is barred, that a gate before unseen has closed, shutting her out from the inner life.

I knew a very advanced woman in Southern India who had broken caste and who went about freely, mingling with both Europeans and Indians with the same freedom as an American woman would. She dressed in a costume partially Indian and partially European, wore slippers, and arranged her hair in the European fashion. One day I went to her house rather earlier than the usual hour for calling. I hardly recognized her, as she was the Indian woman of the home, dressed in a sari, her hair hanging down her back in braids, and with heavy anklets over her bare feet. She blushed and said: " Oh, I do not want you to see me like this," and she did not understand me when I told her that I felt that I was seeing the real woman for the first time.

I thought many times in my long residence in the East that I had really entered into the life and understood the thoughts, hopes, and ambitions of the Eastern woman, when at some thoughtless word or action on my part a wall of fog would come between us, with a thick, impenetrable, blanket-like mist, made up of custom, tradition, and the results of environment, and when it would lift we would find our little boats far from each other on a sea of mutual misunderstanding.

Despite our incapacity to enter into the soul life of this ancient East, we find ourselves fascinated and bewitched by the charm of these secluded women of the Orient, who live a life of instinctive unselfishness, their days given to the making of happiness for others.

We say : " Must there always remain the width of the world between the Eastern woman and the woman of the West? Will the education which is being grasped so eagerly by the woman of the Orient lessen the distance, and will it break down the barriers?" Only time will tell. The children of the present boys and girls in school and college will have had the foundation of the three generations of intellectual training, and will have learned to take what is best for them from Western knowledge and use it as a means of breaking the iron bands of ignorance, superstition, and loyalty to old-time custom and tradition, which stands an immovable mountain in the pathway of true friendship between the woman of the West and the woman of the East.